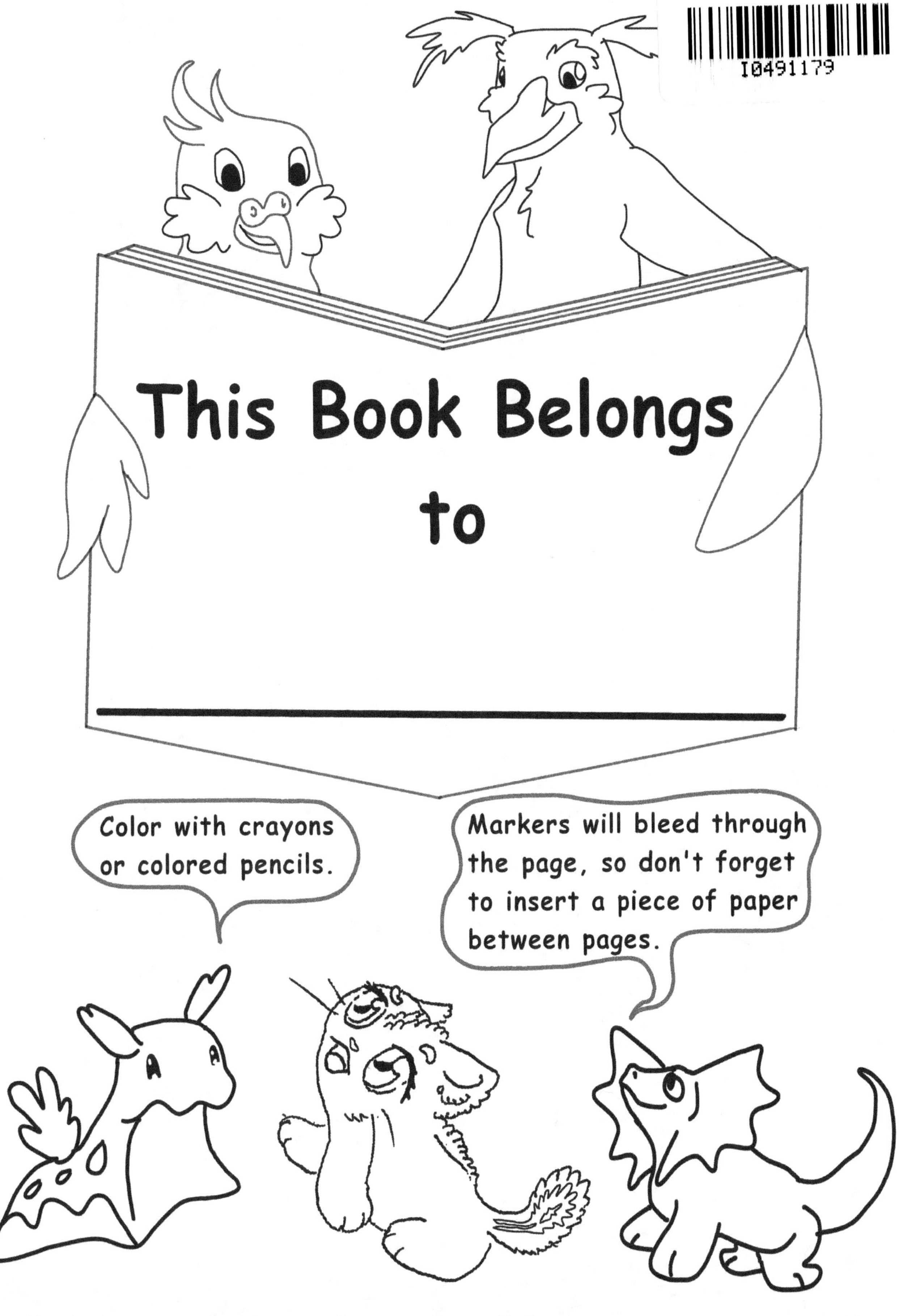
This Book Belongs
to
Color with crayons or colored pencils.
Markers will bleed through the page, so don't forget to insert a piece of paper between pages.

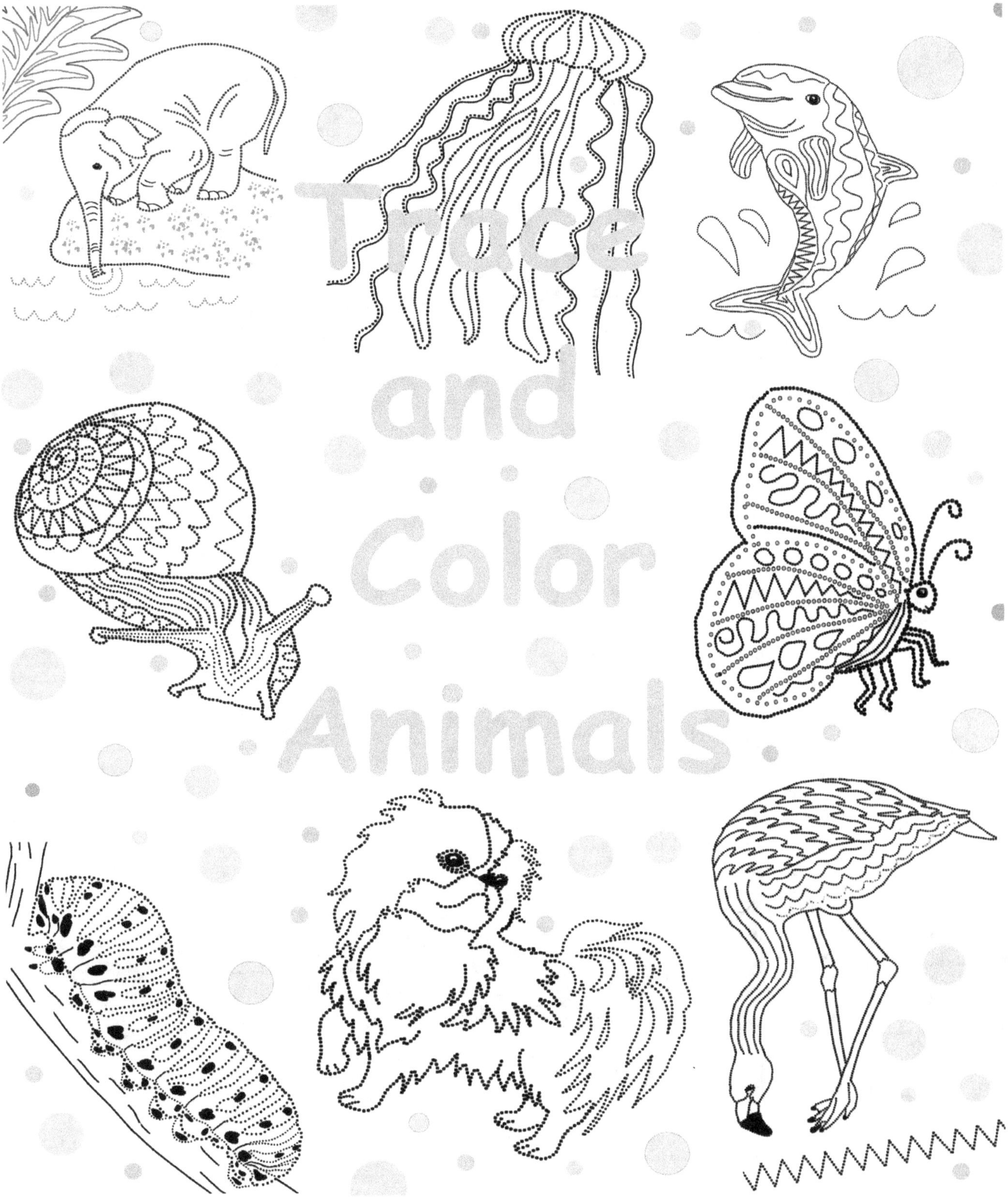
Trace
and
Color
Animals

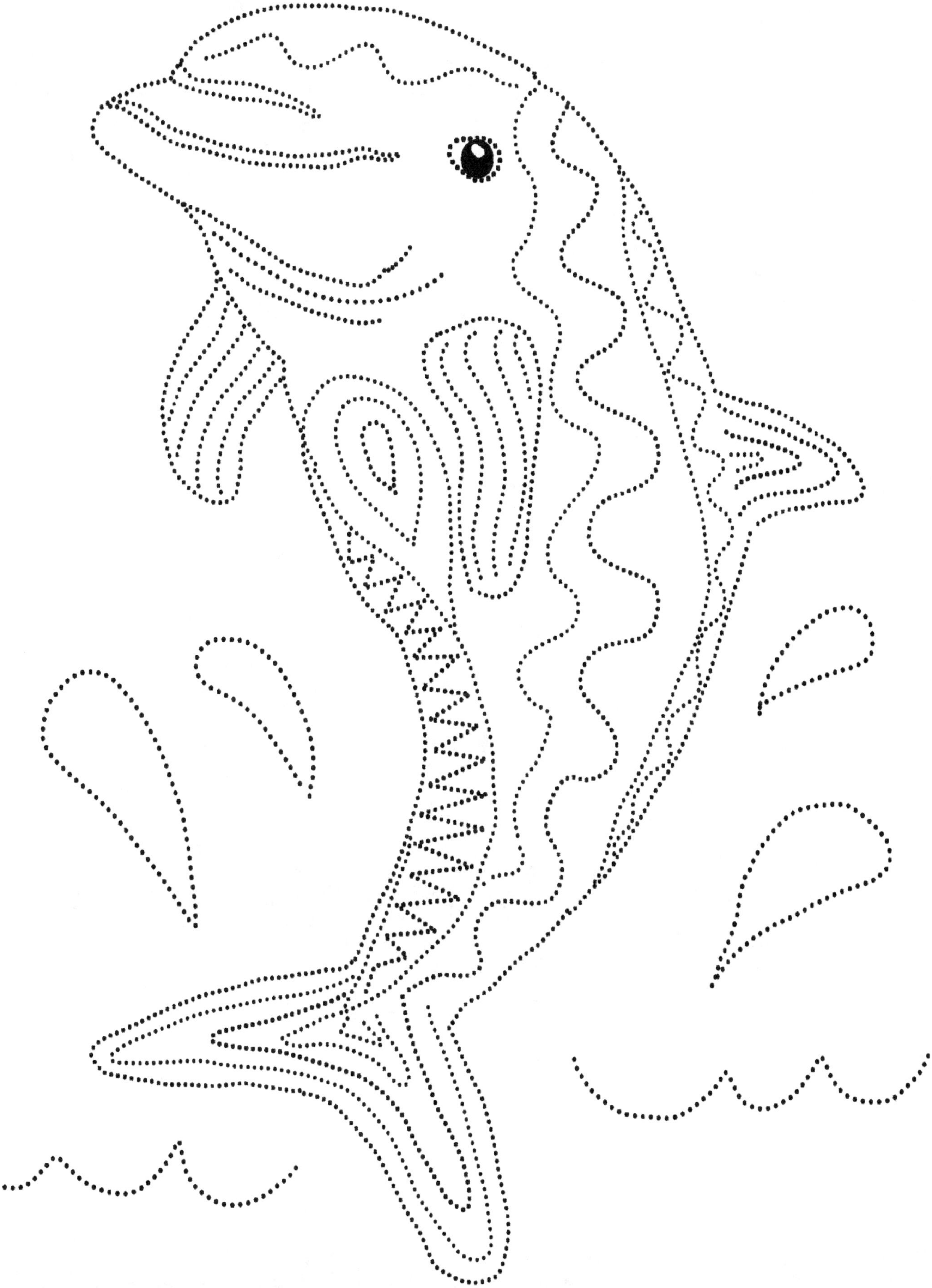

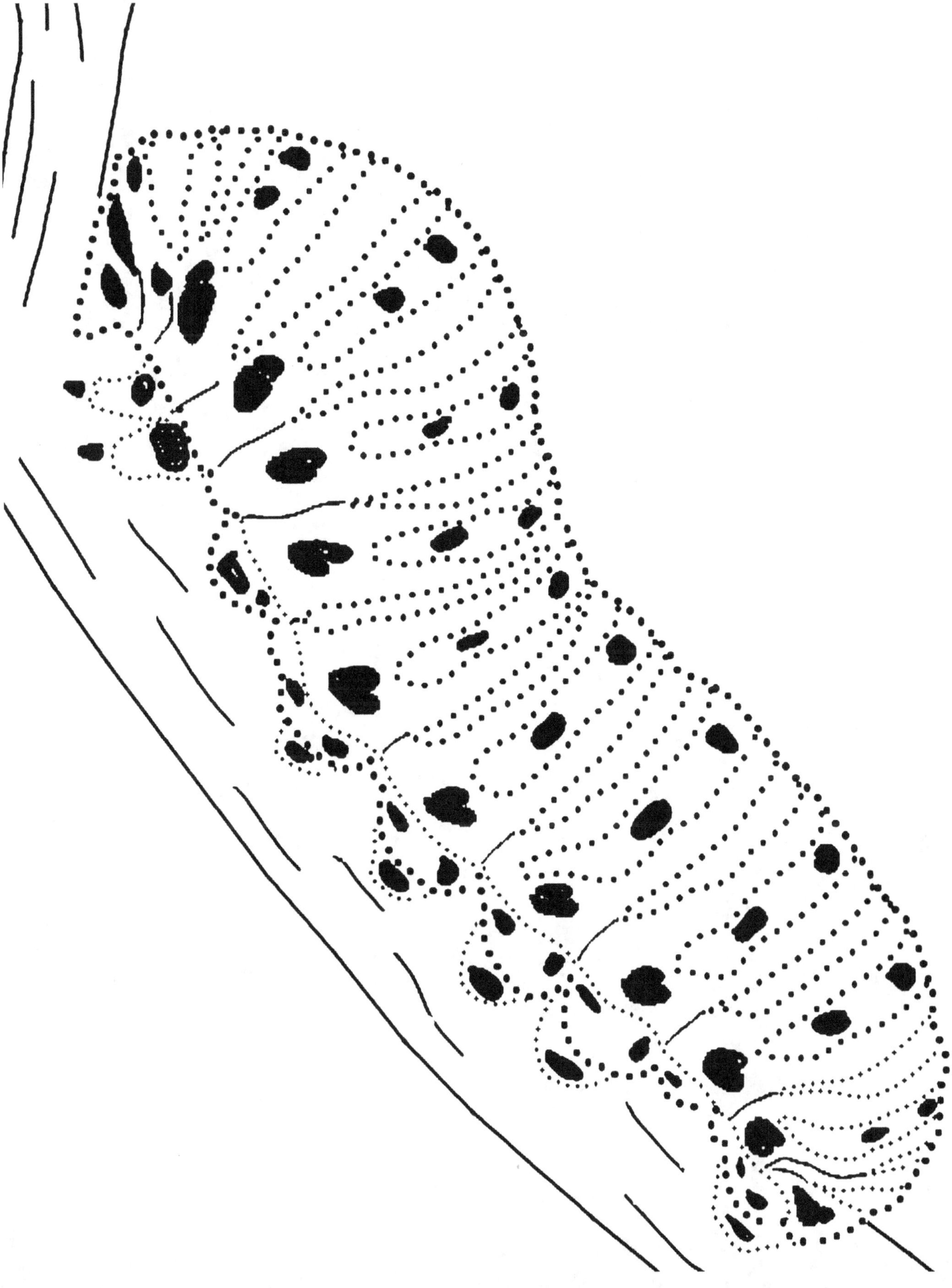

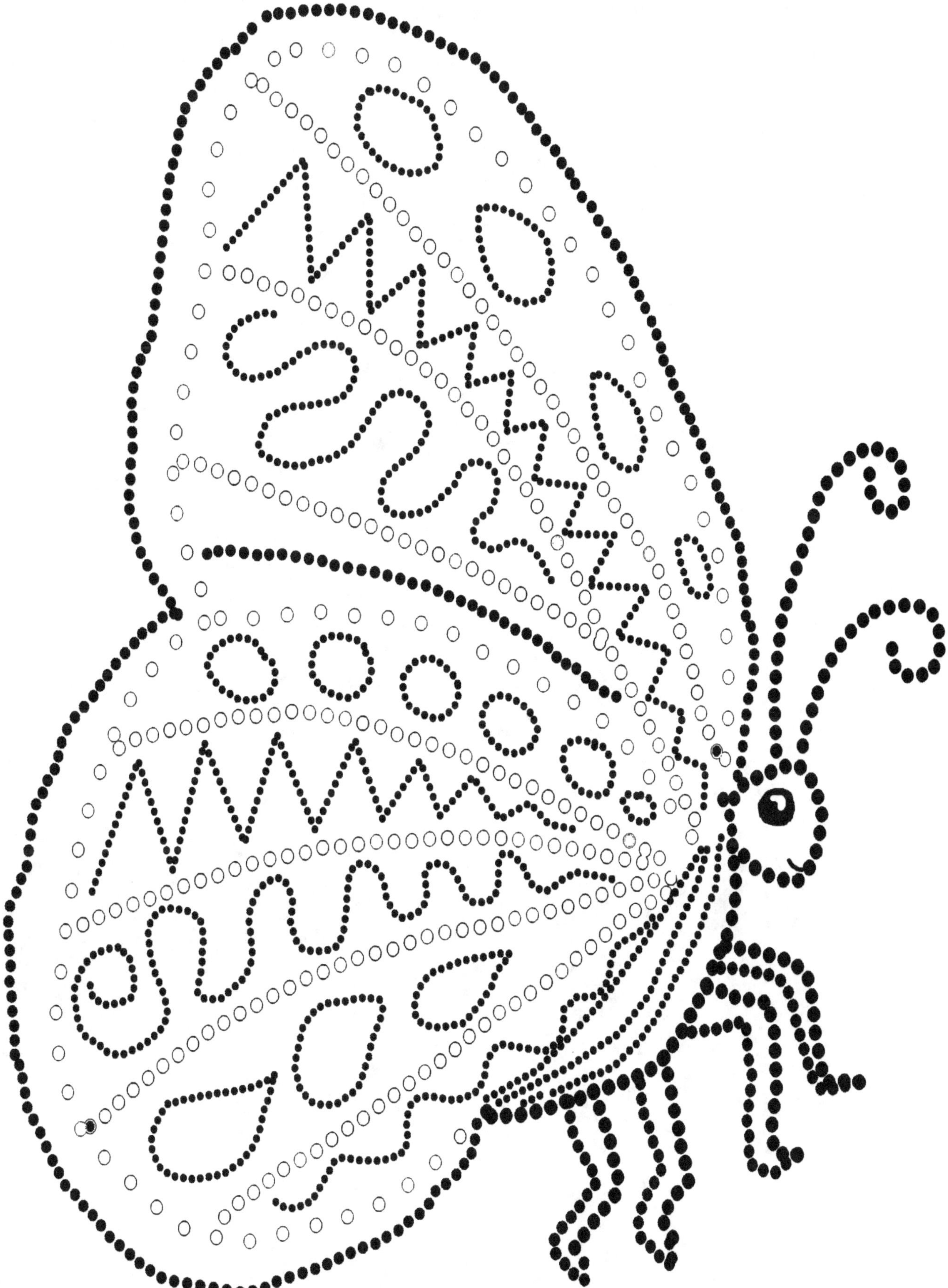

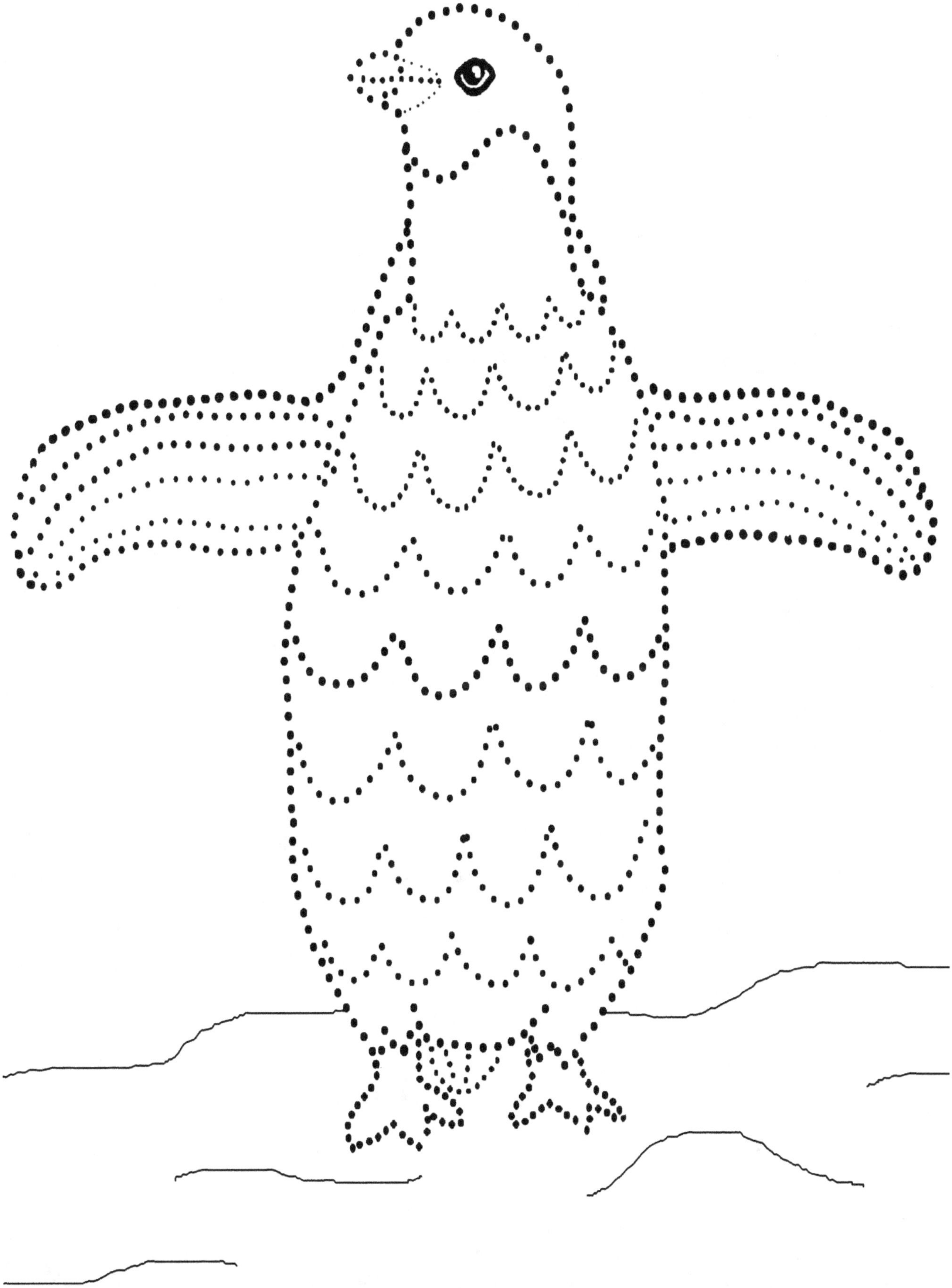

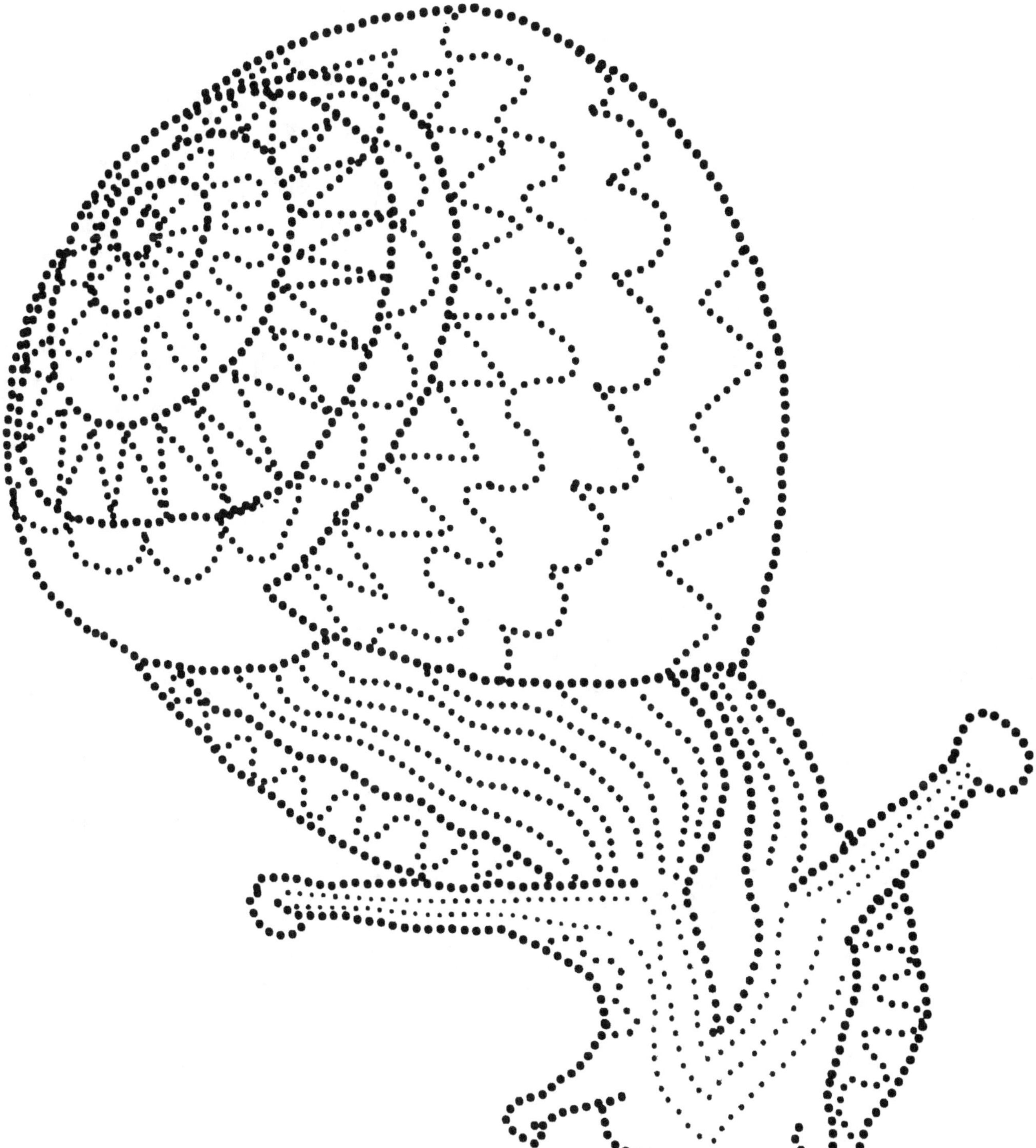

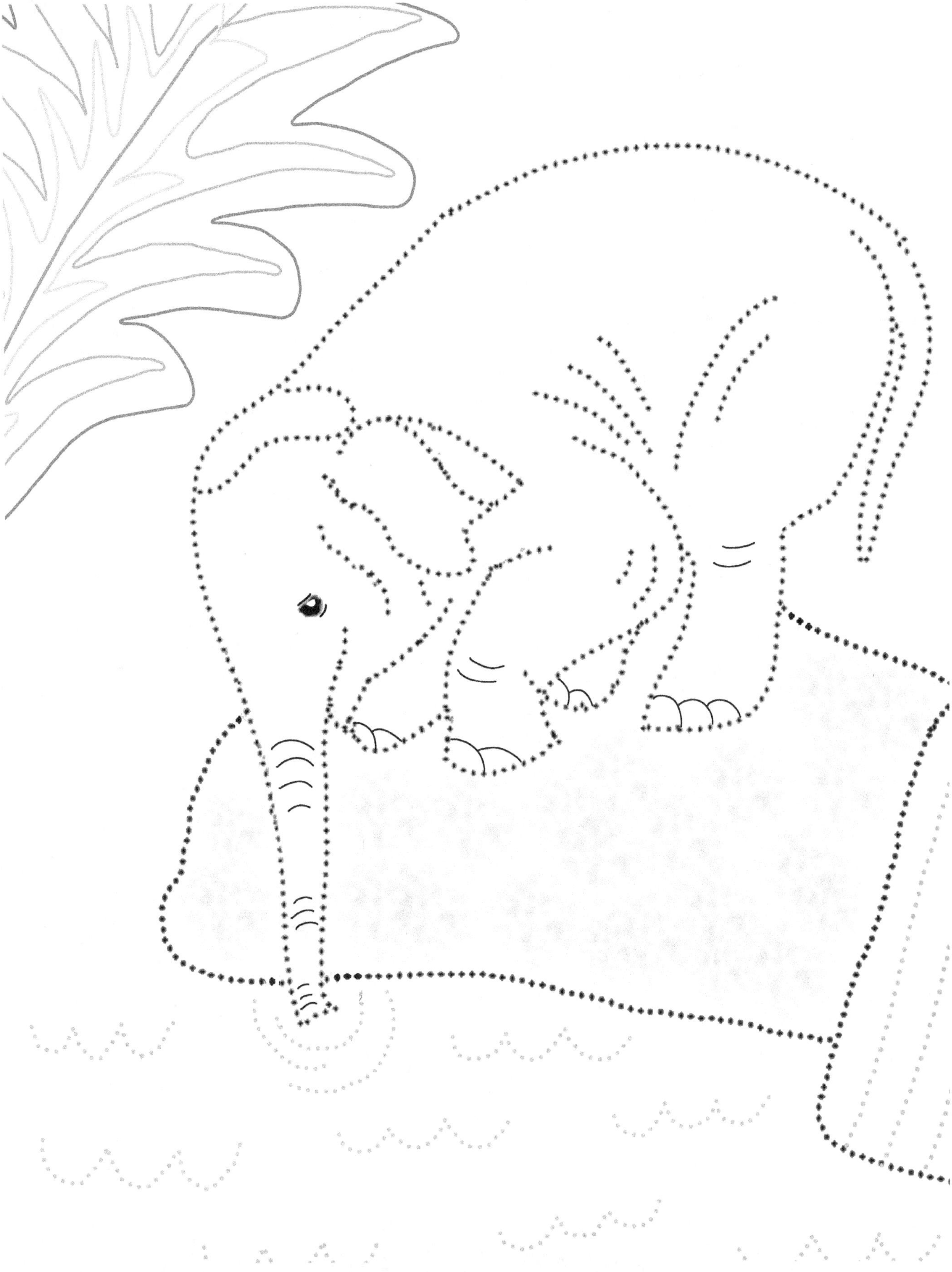

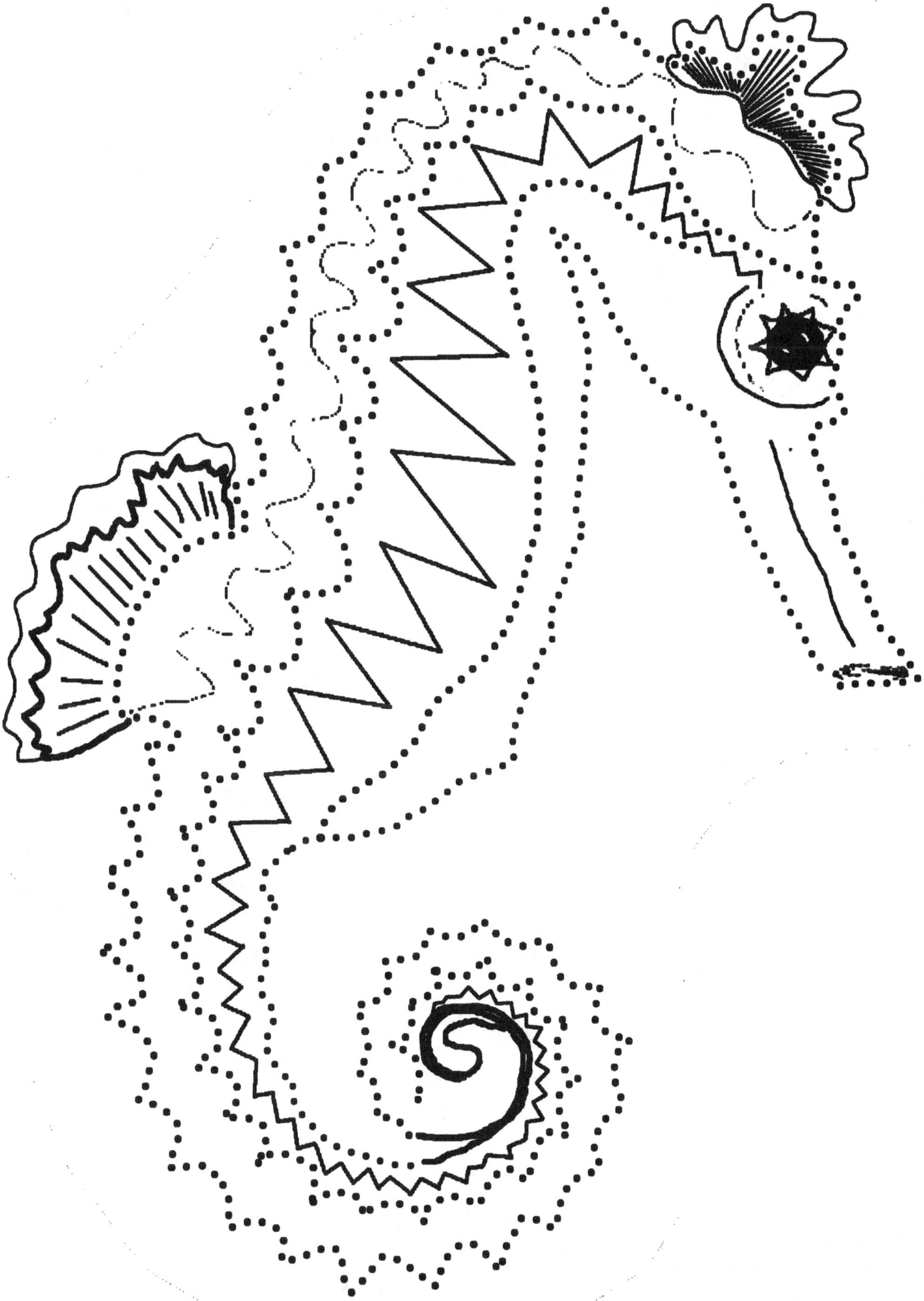

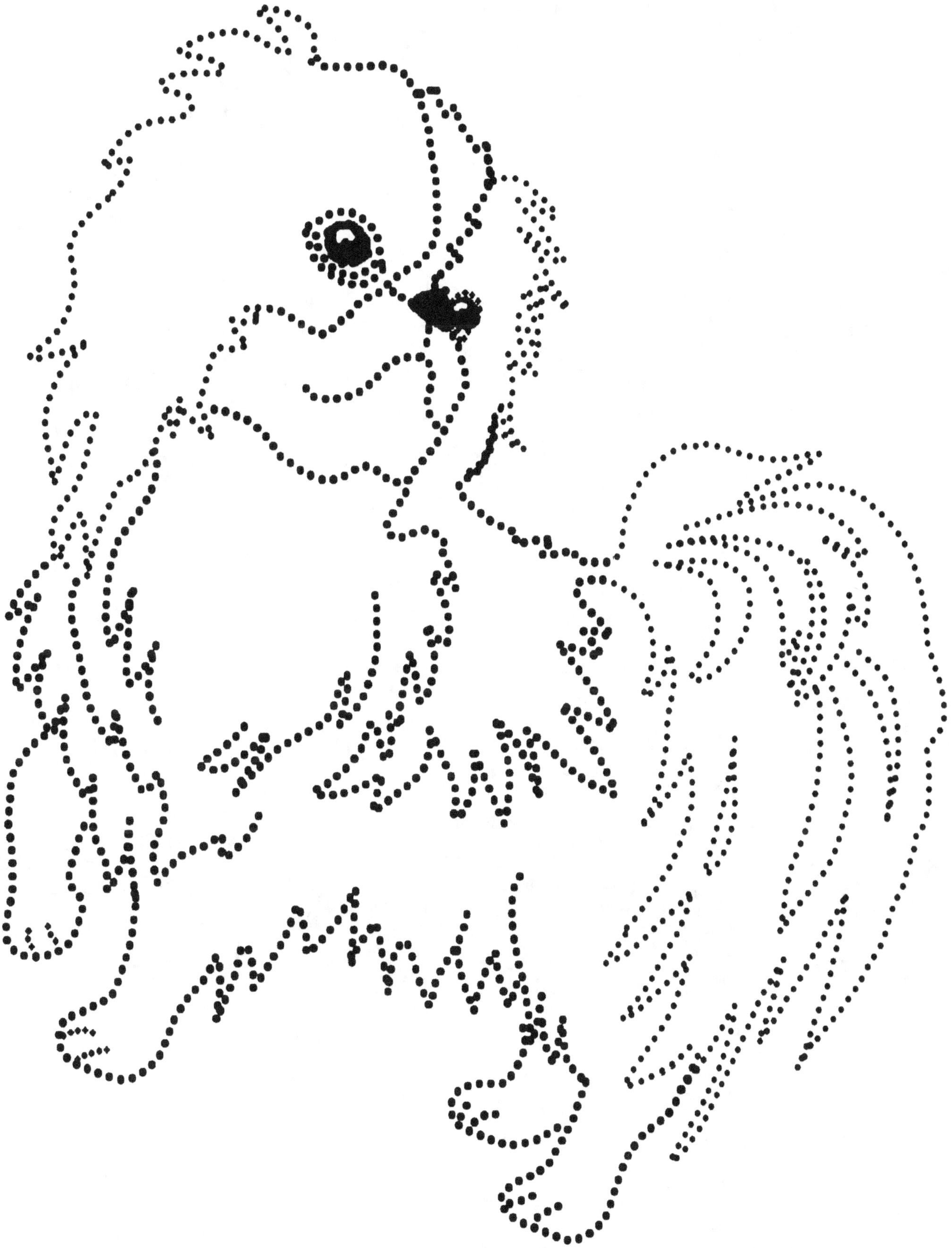

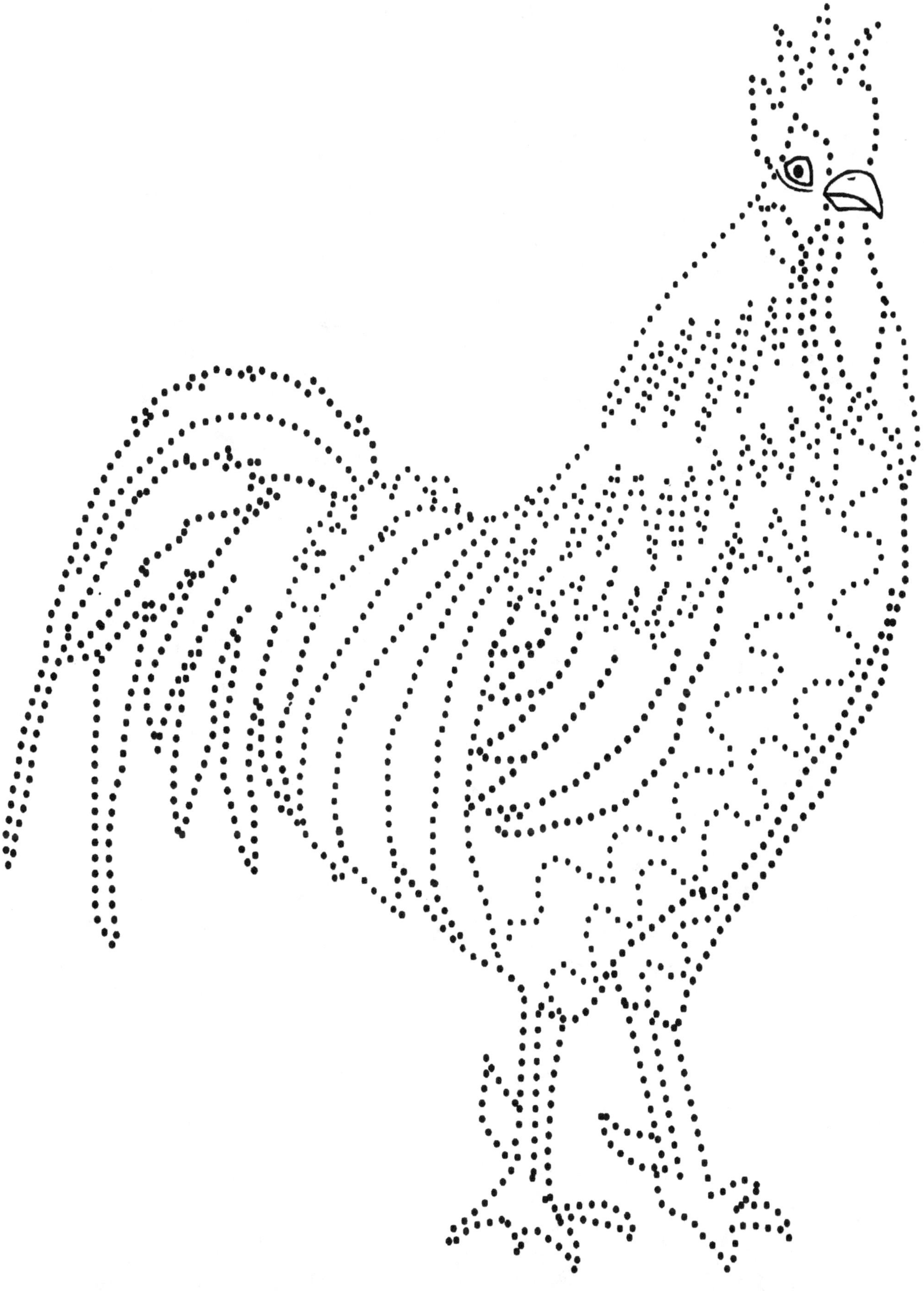

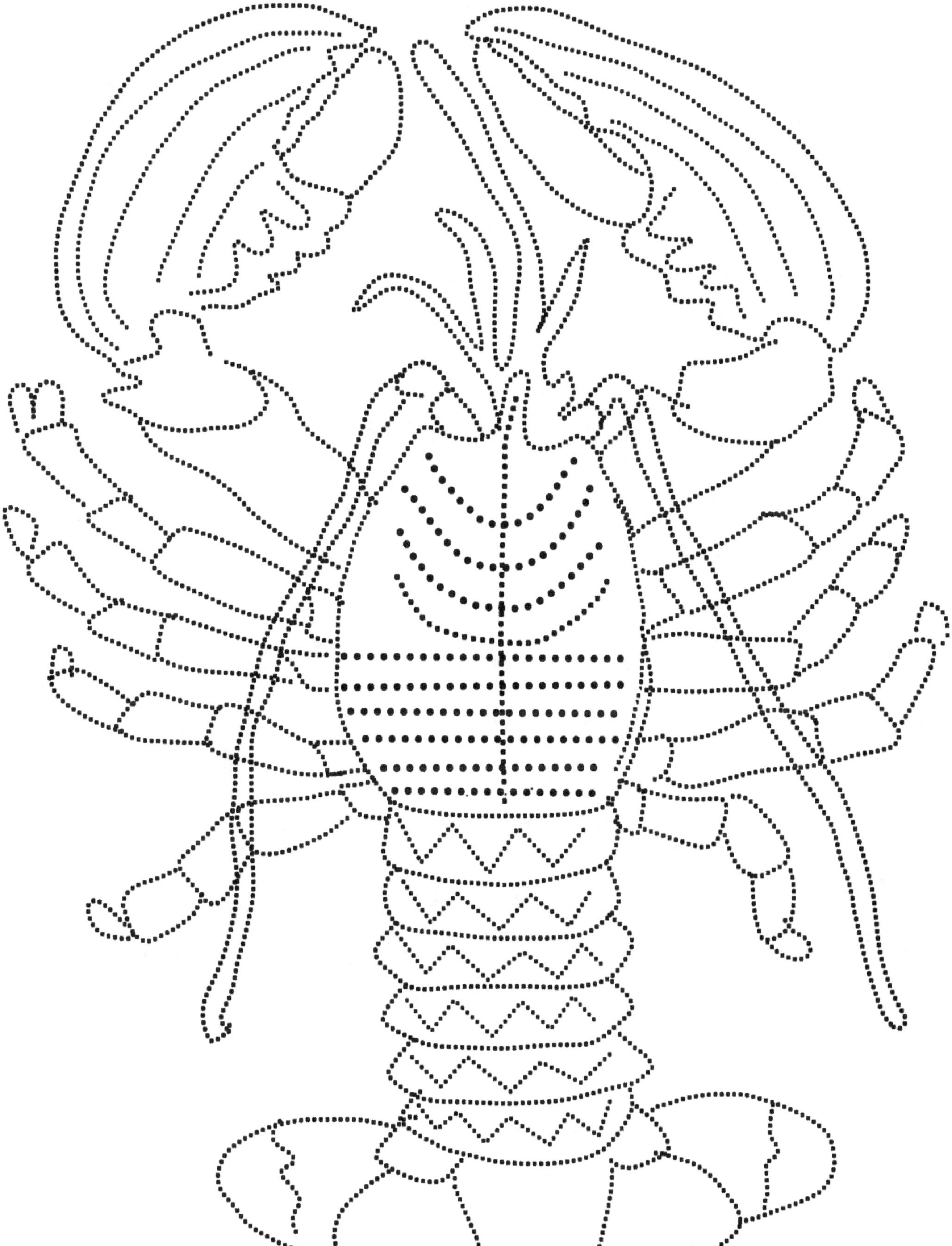

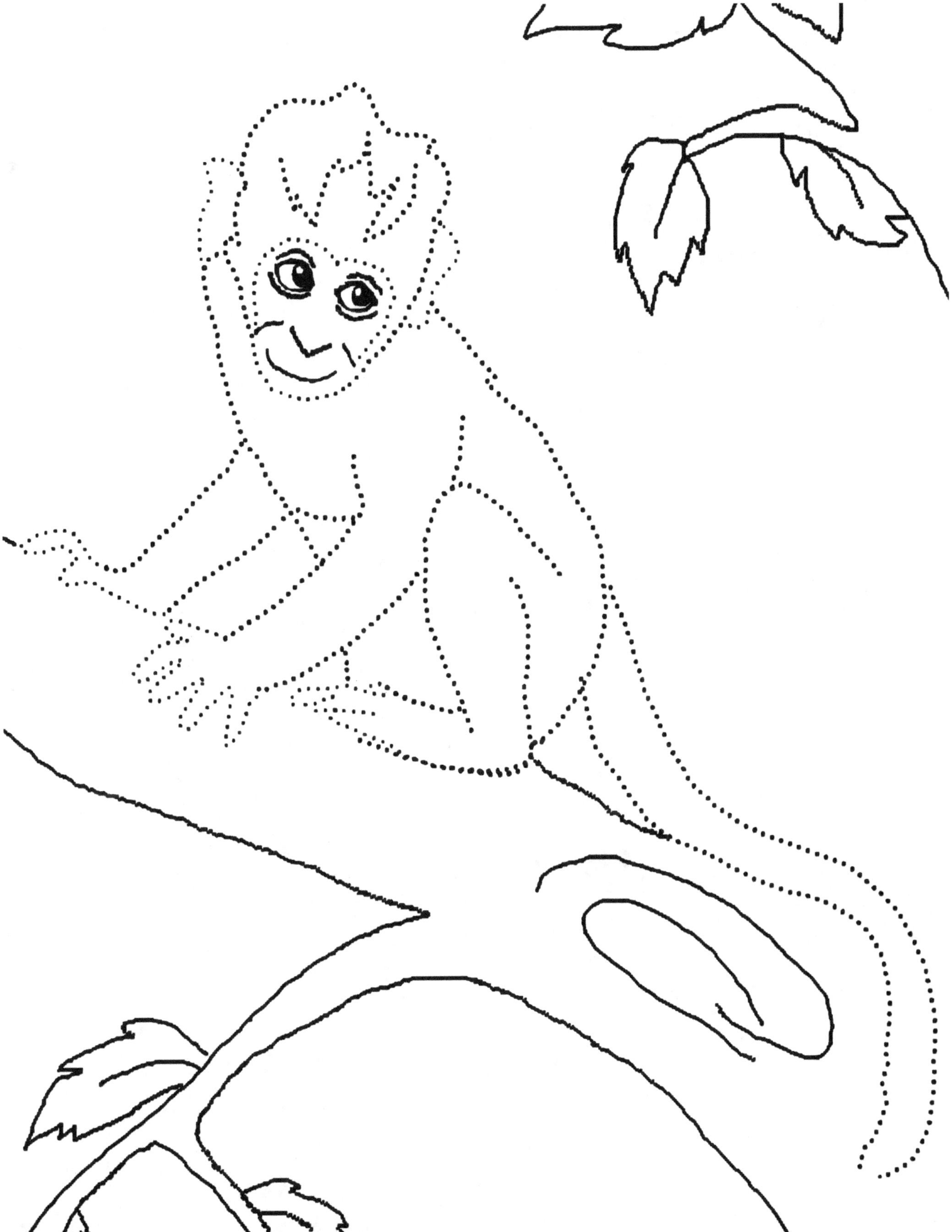

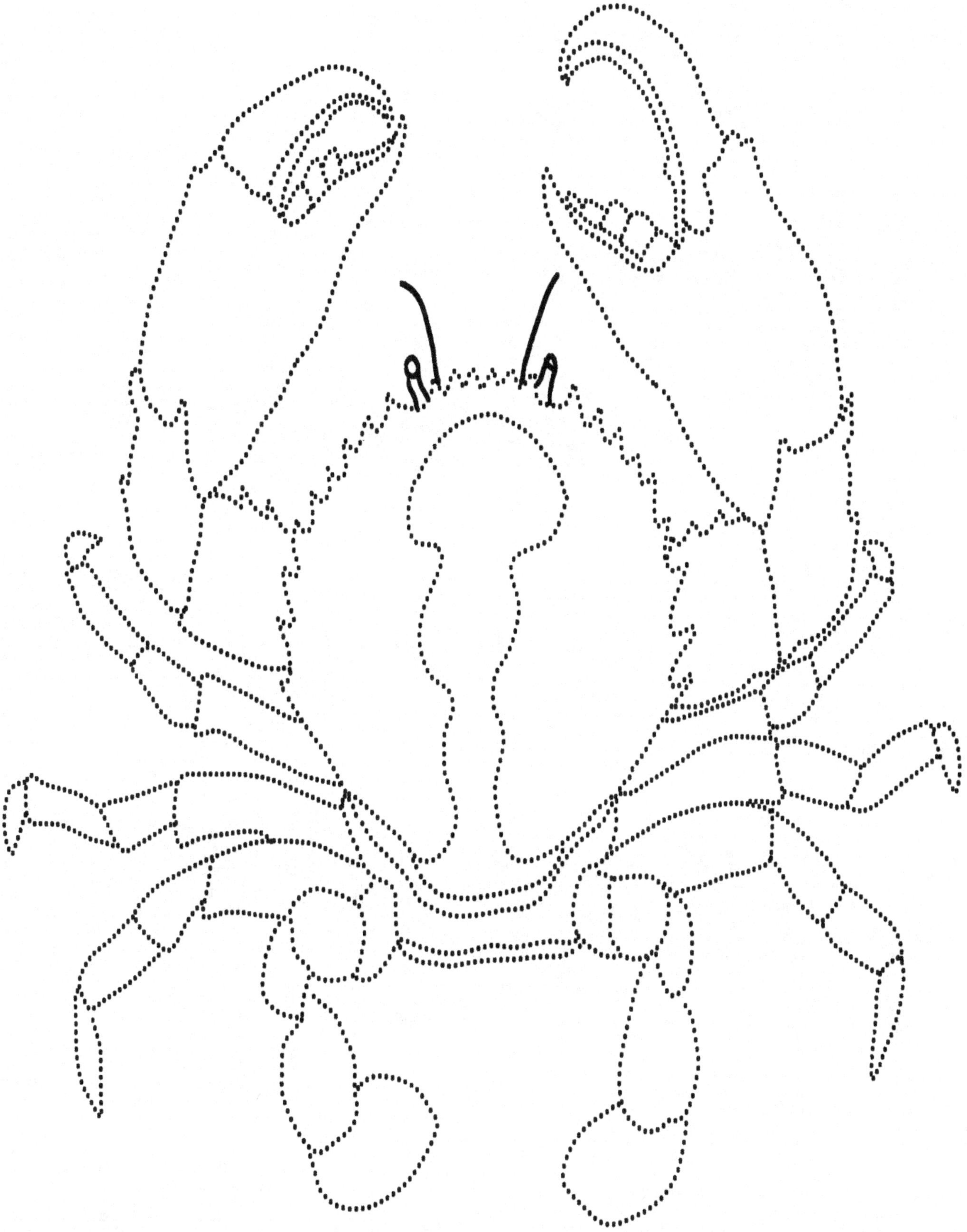

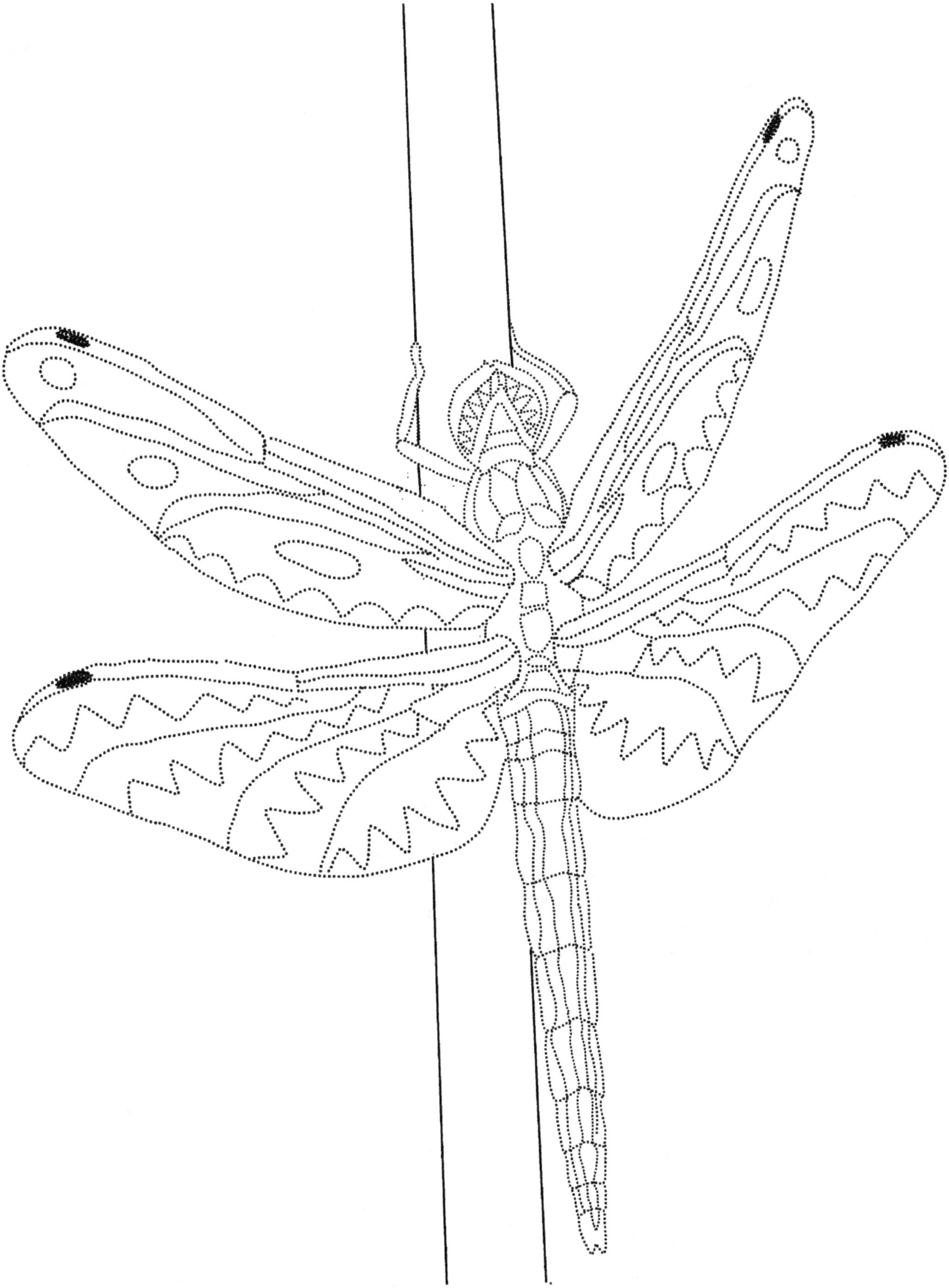

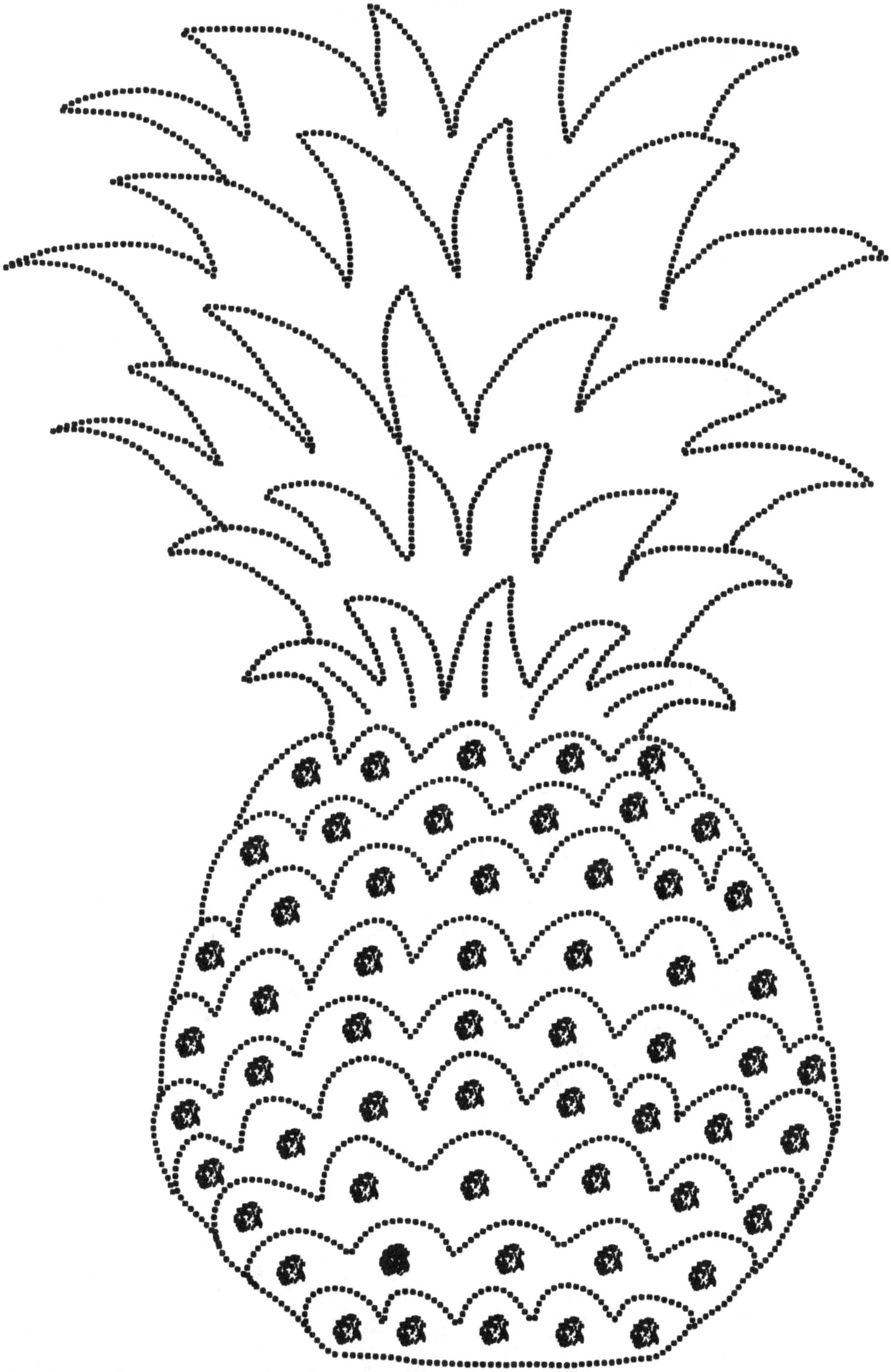

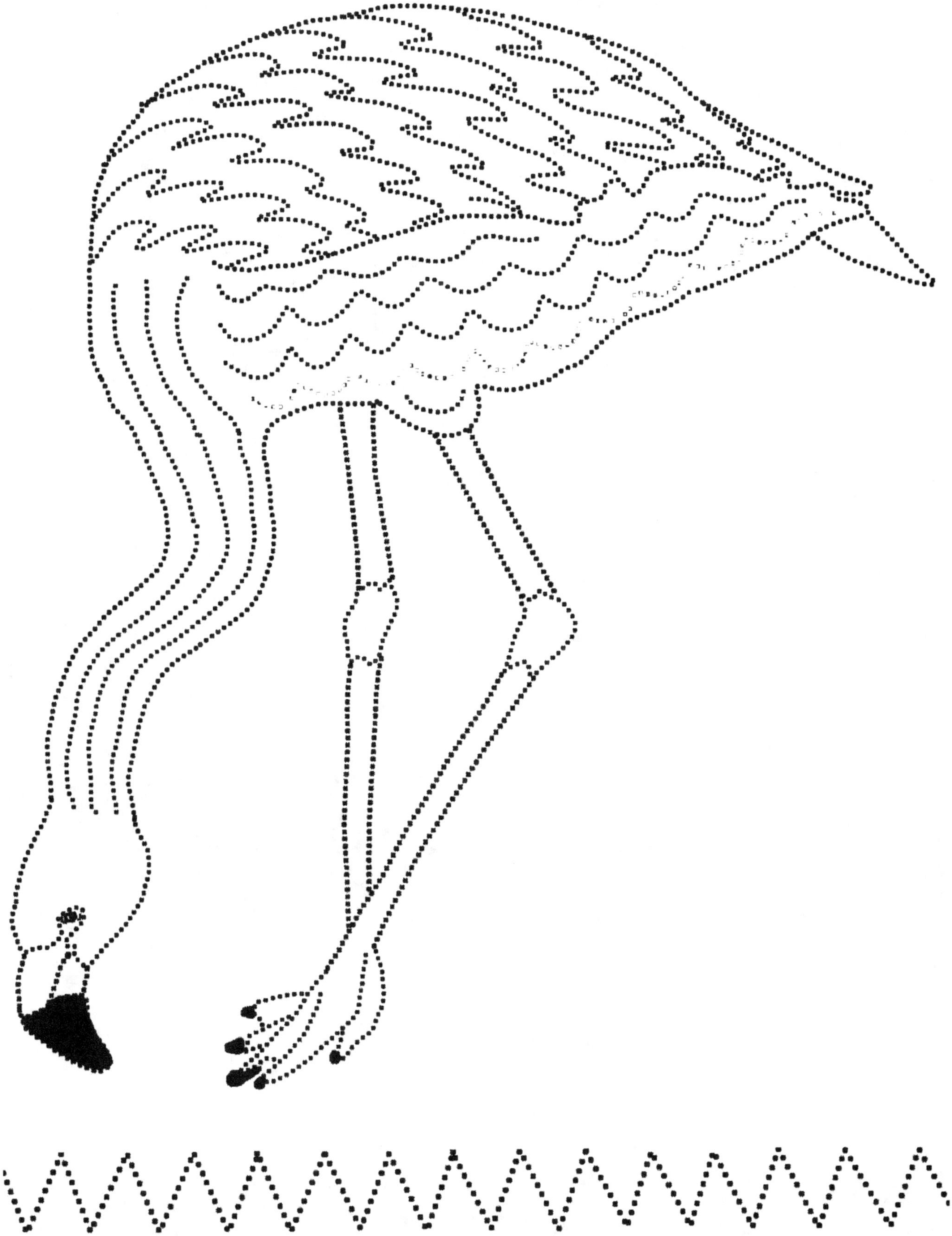

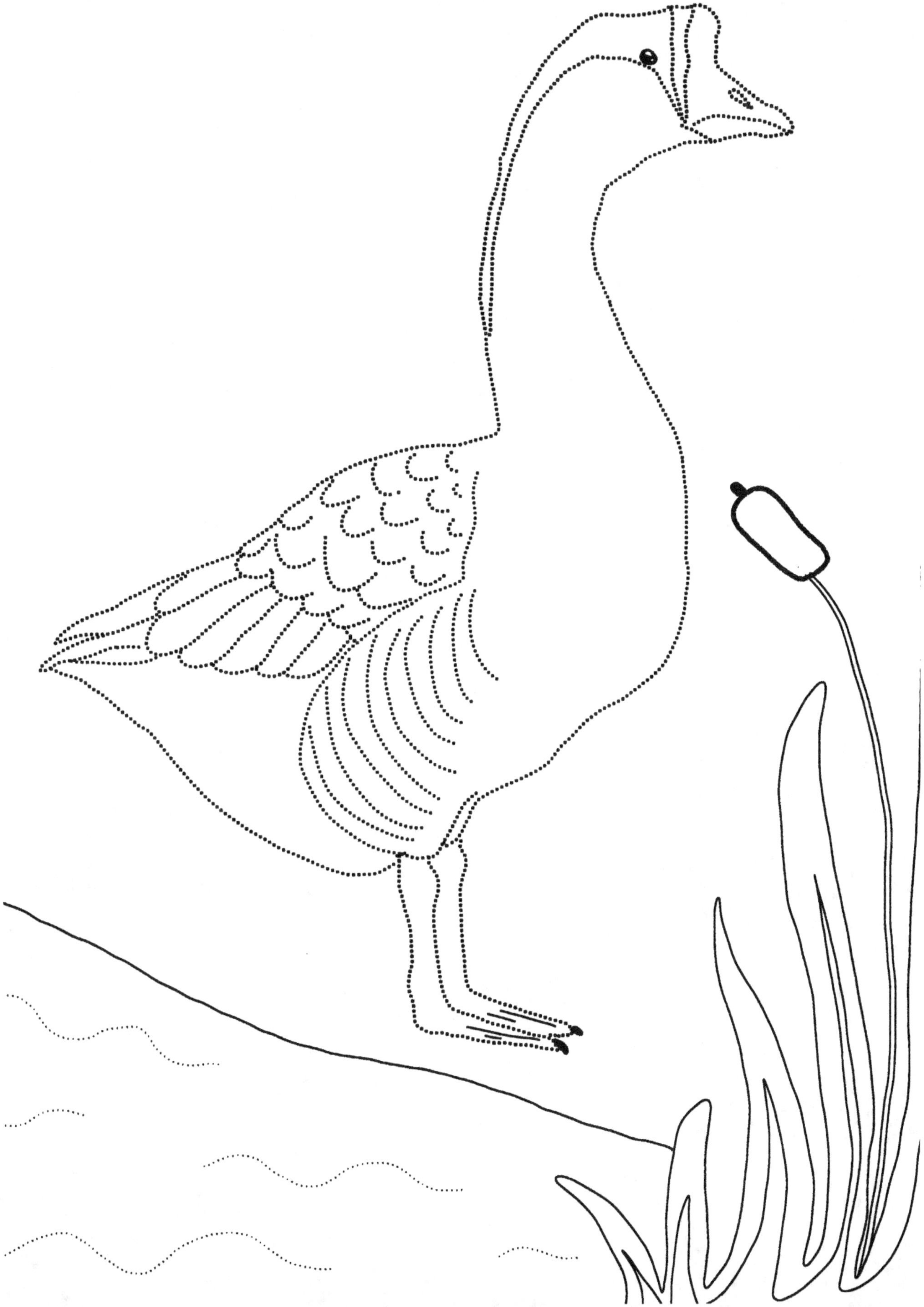

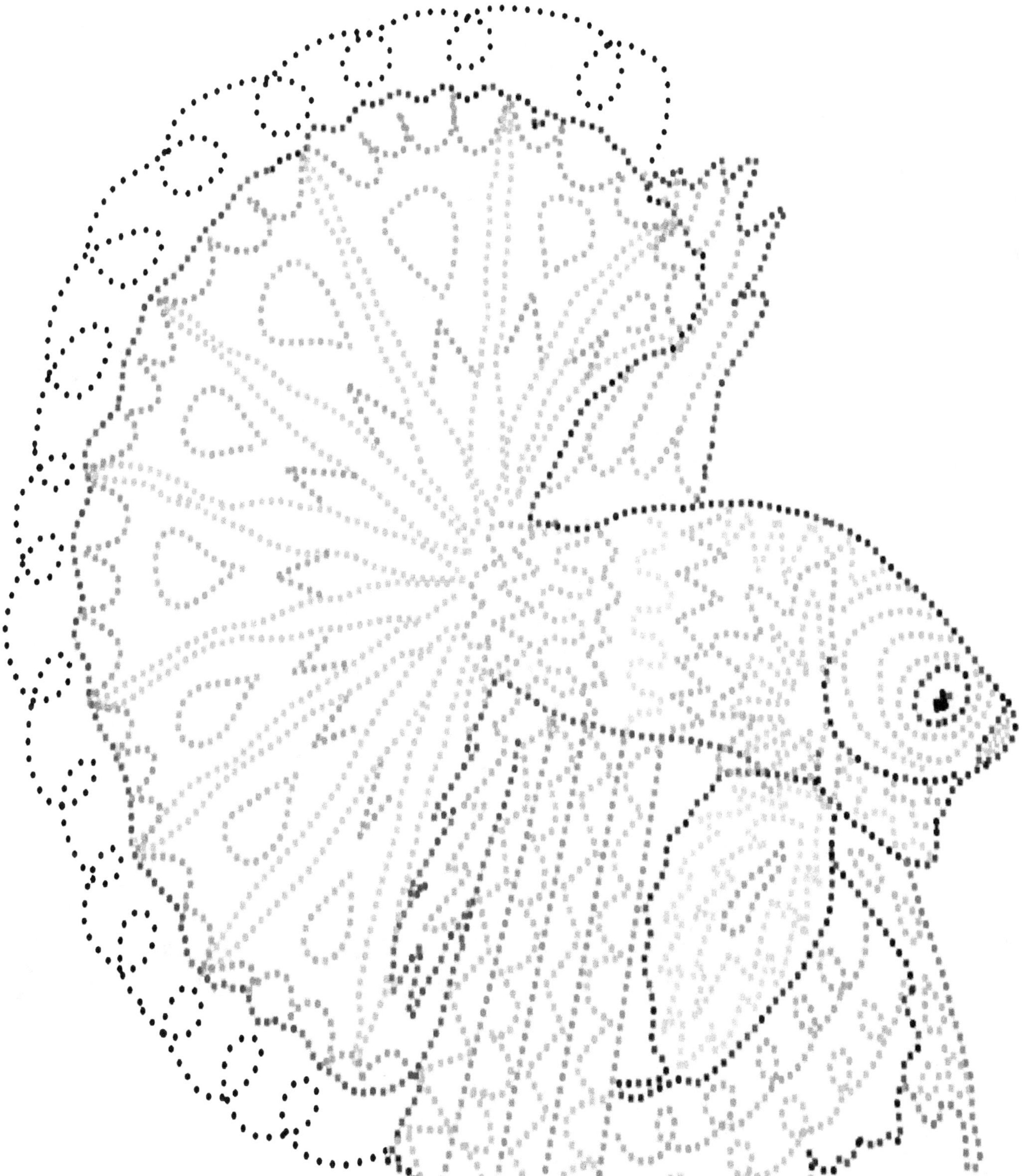

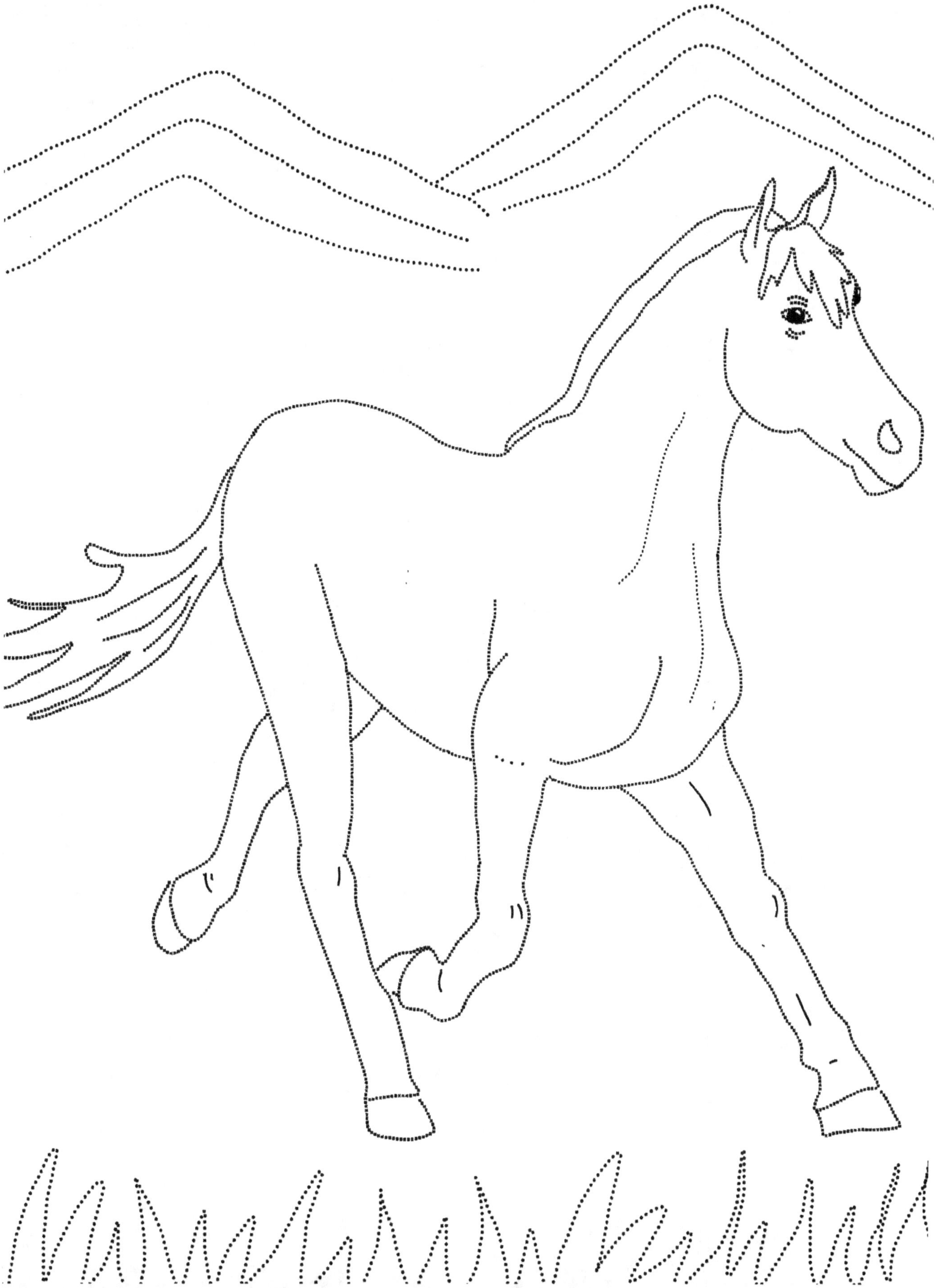

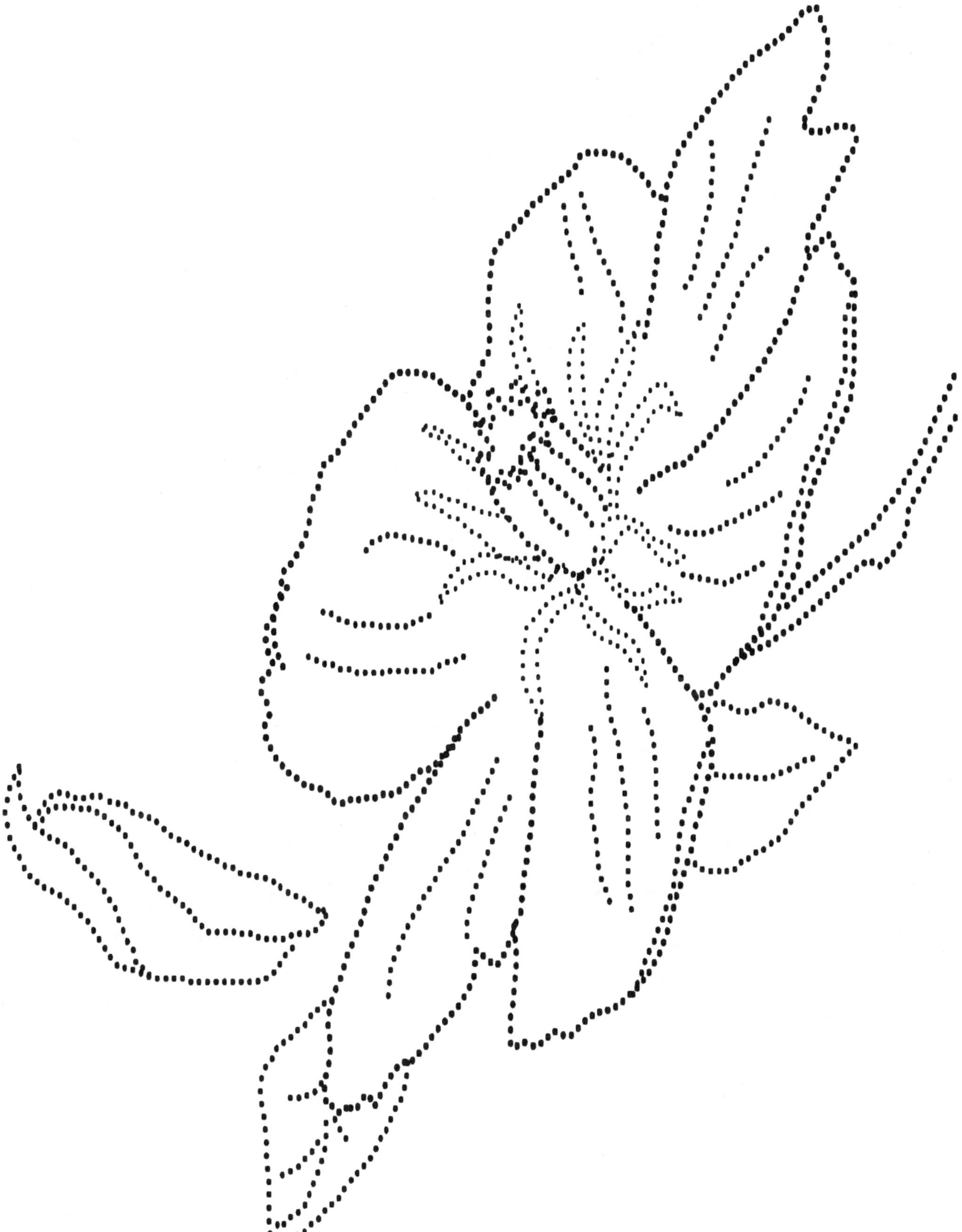

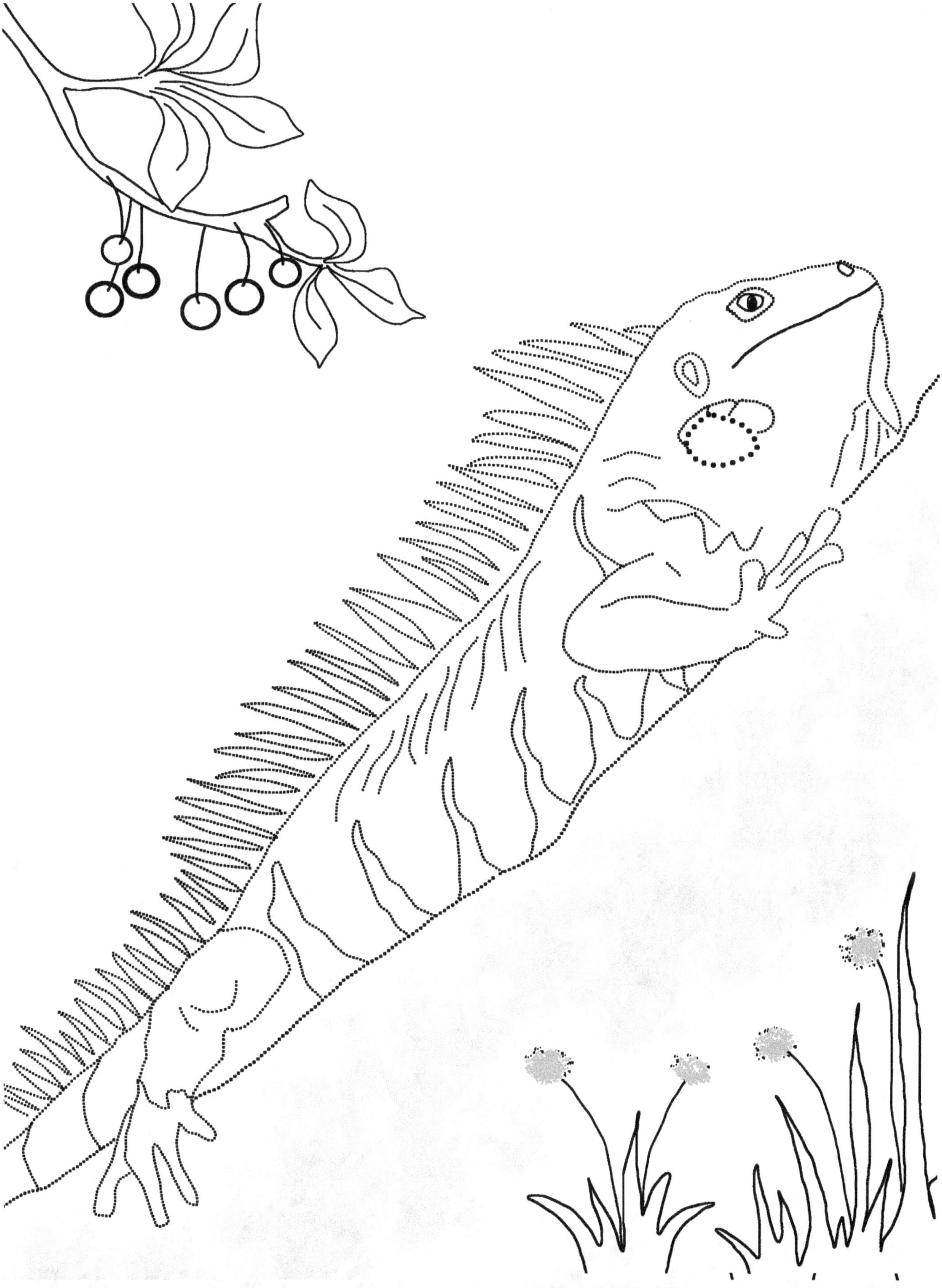

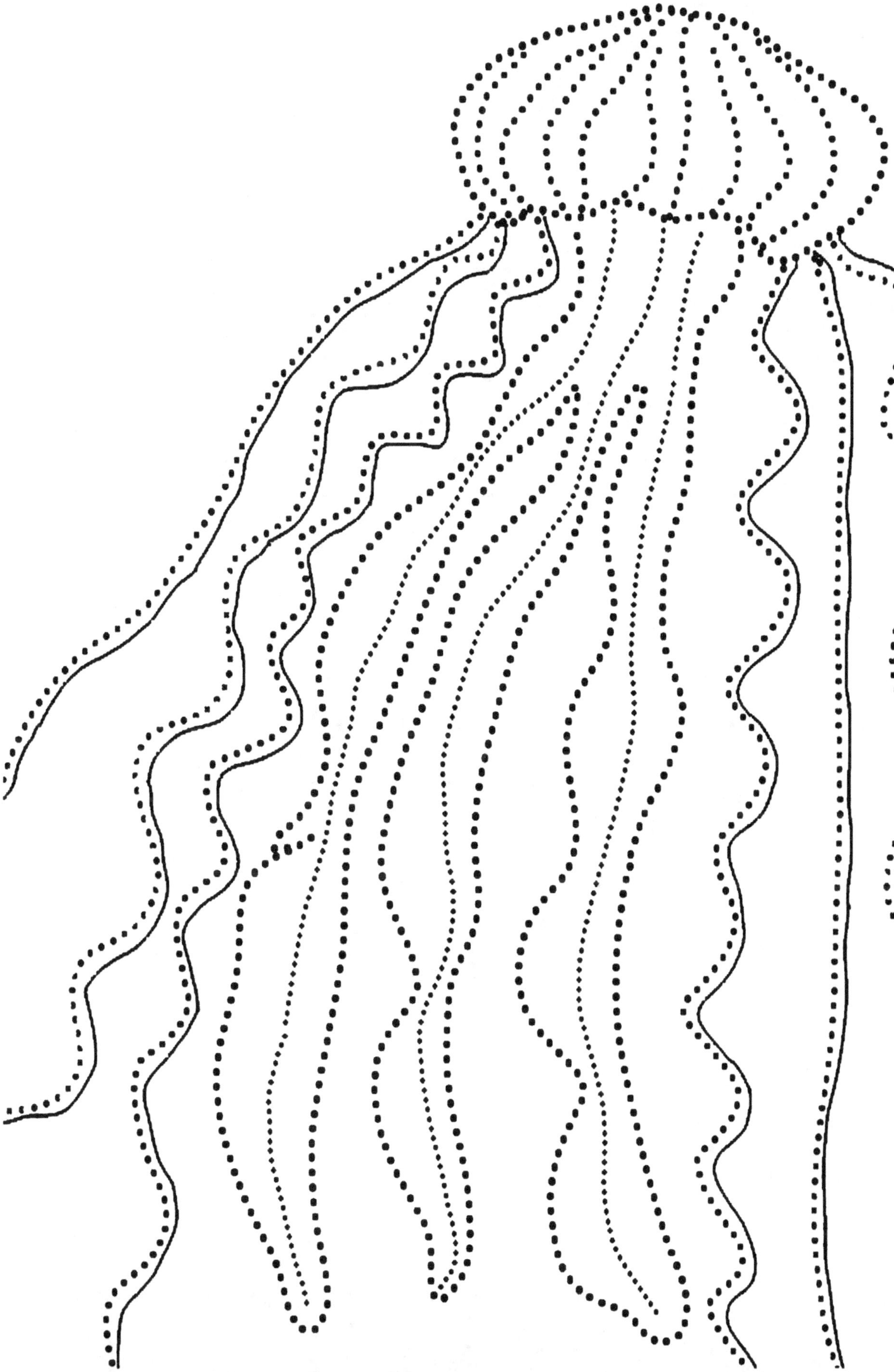

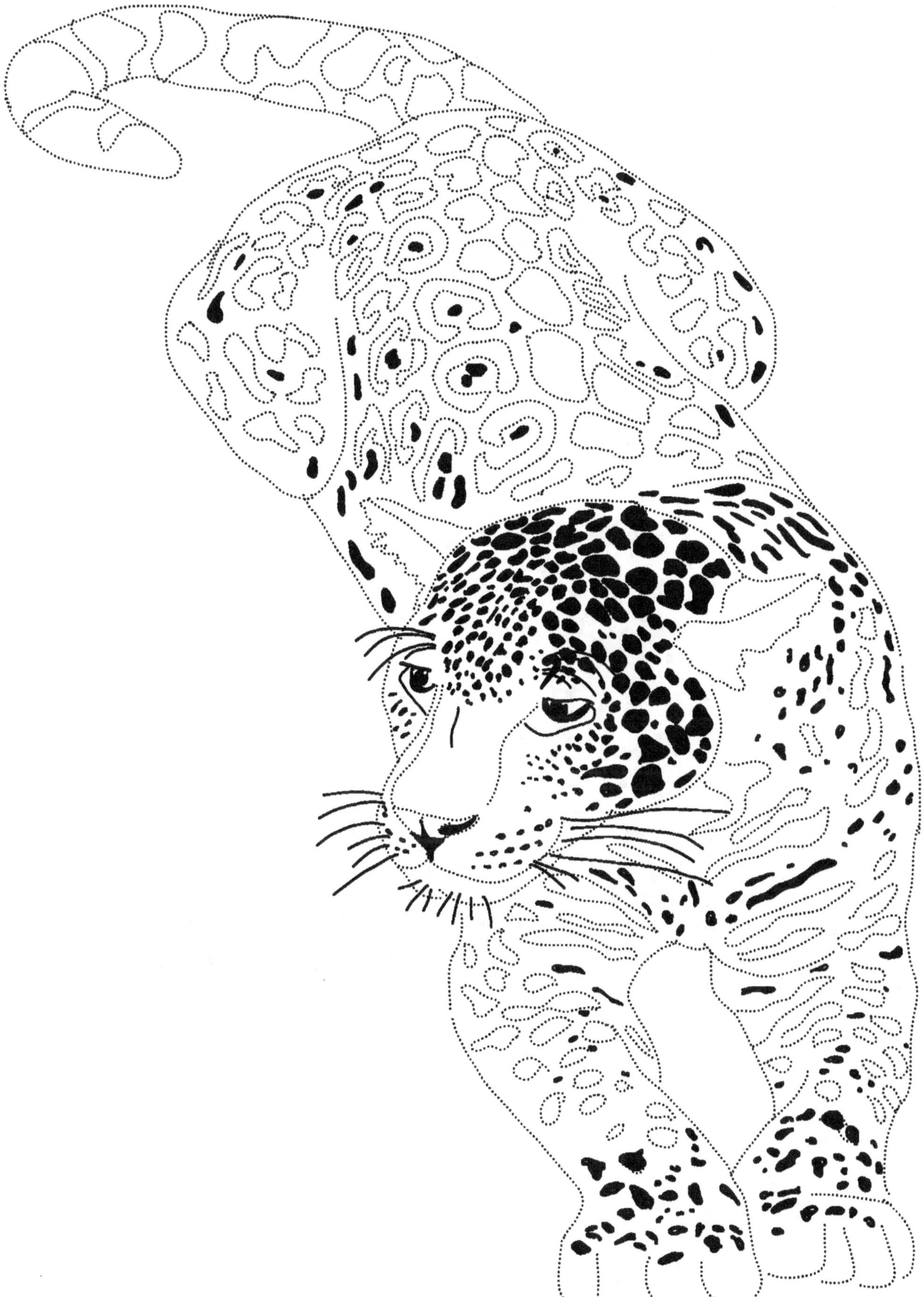

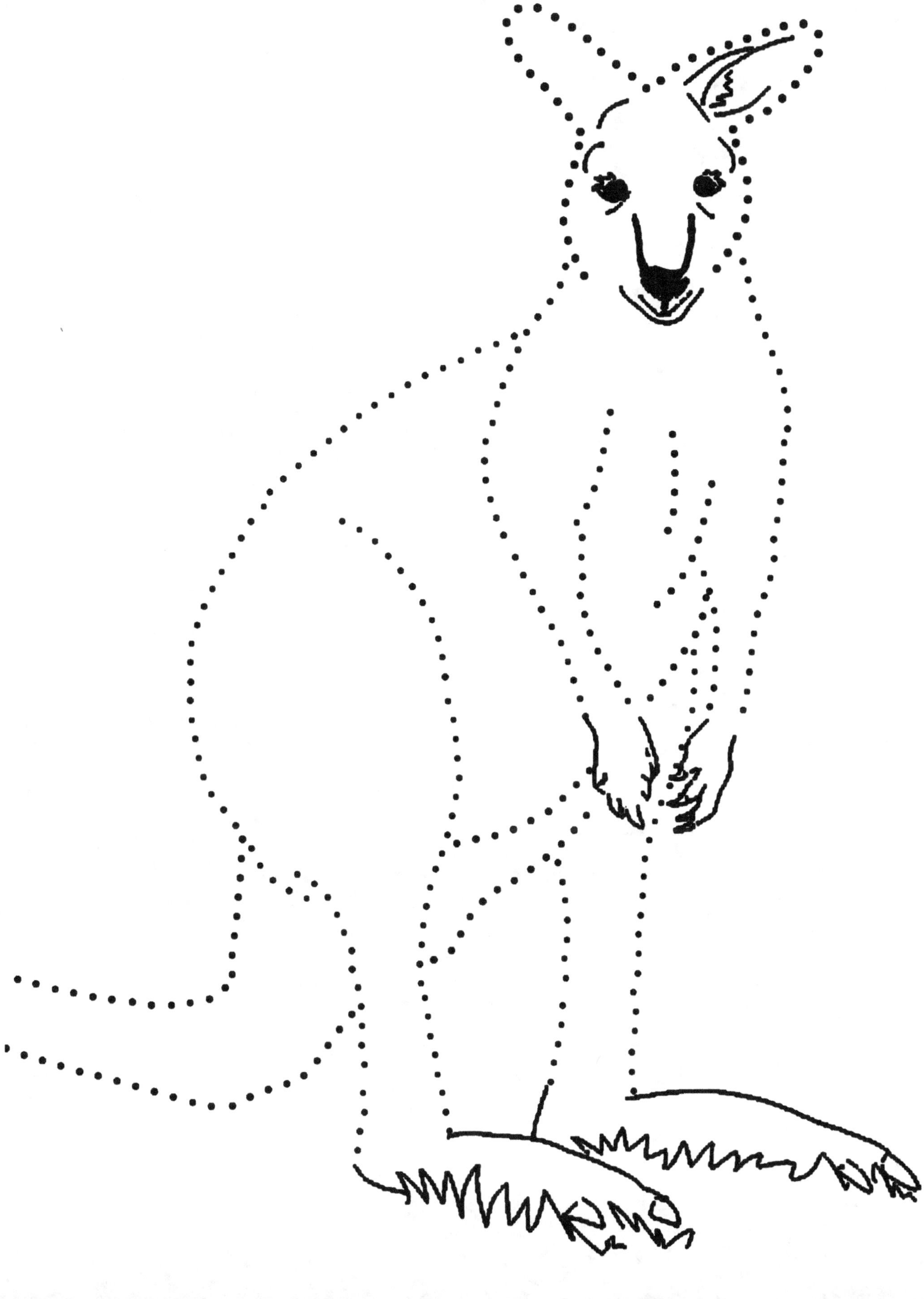

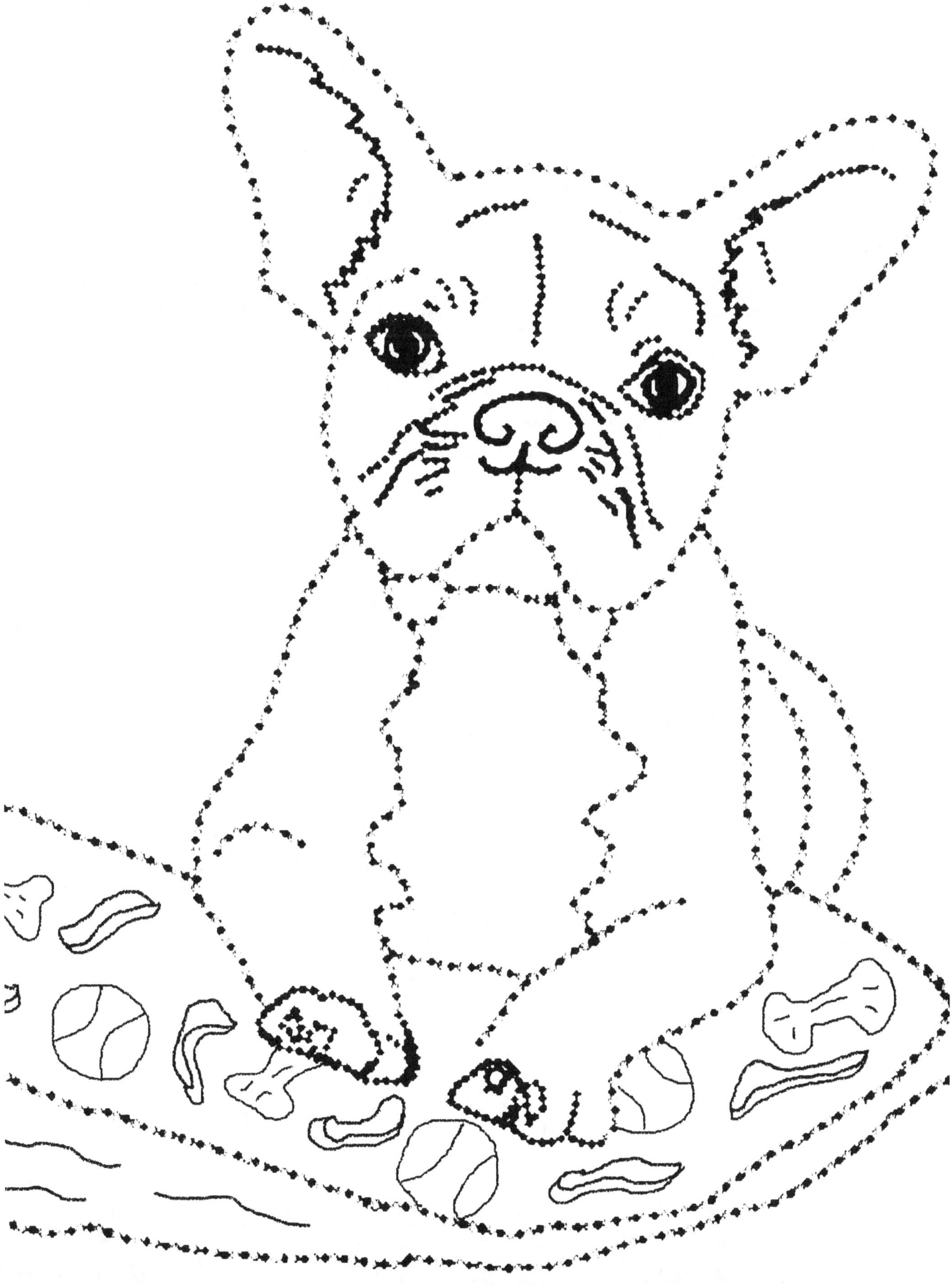

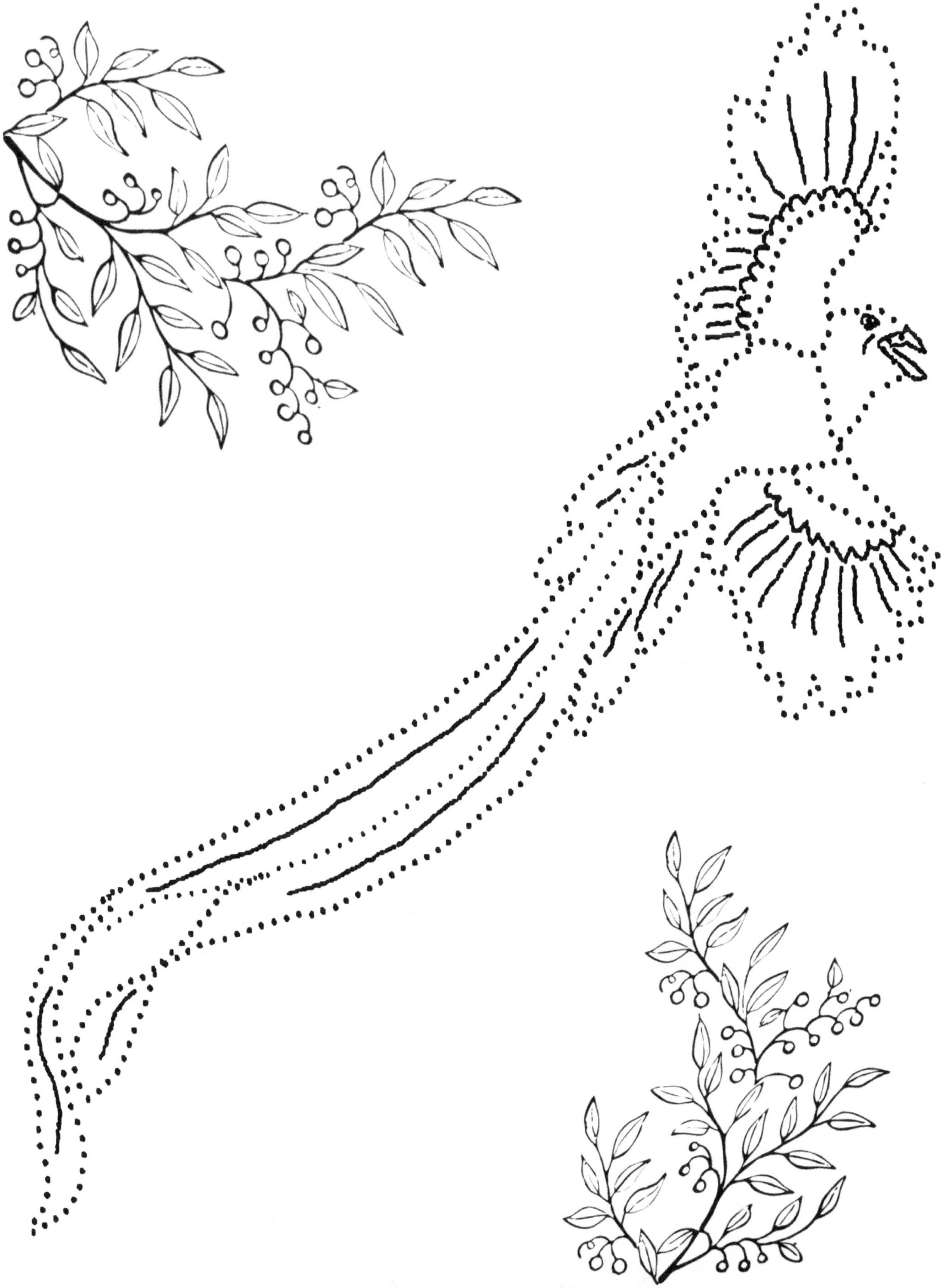

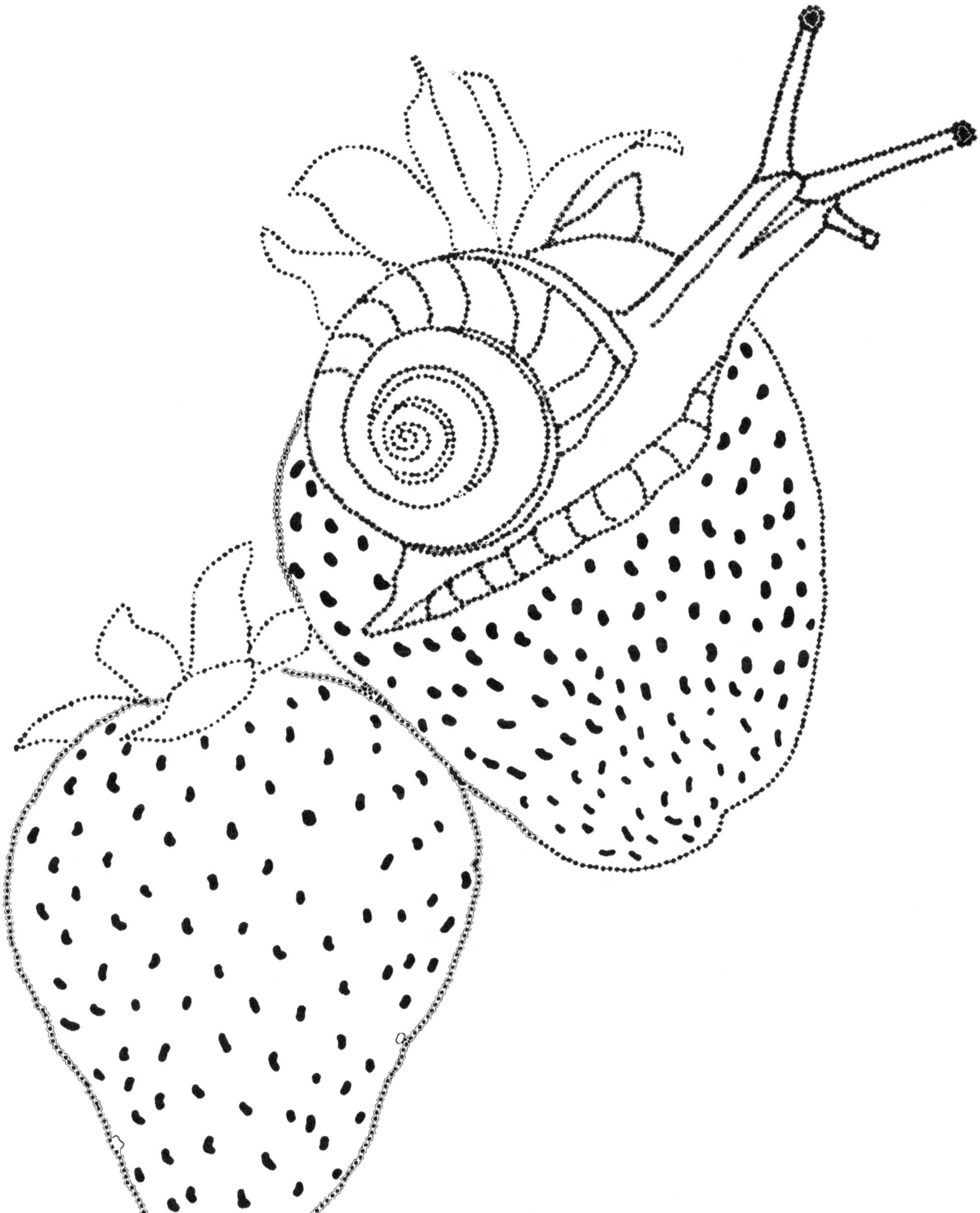

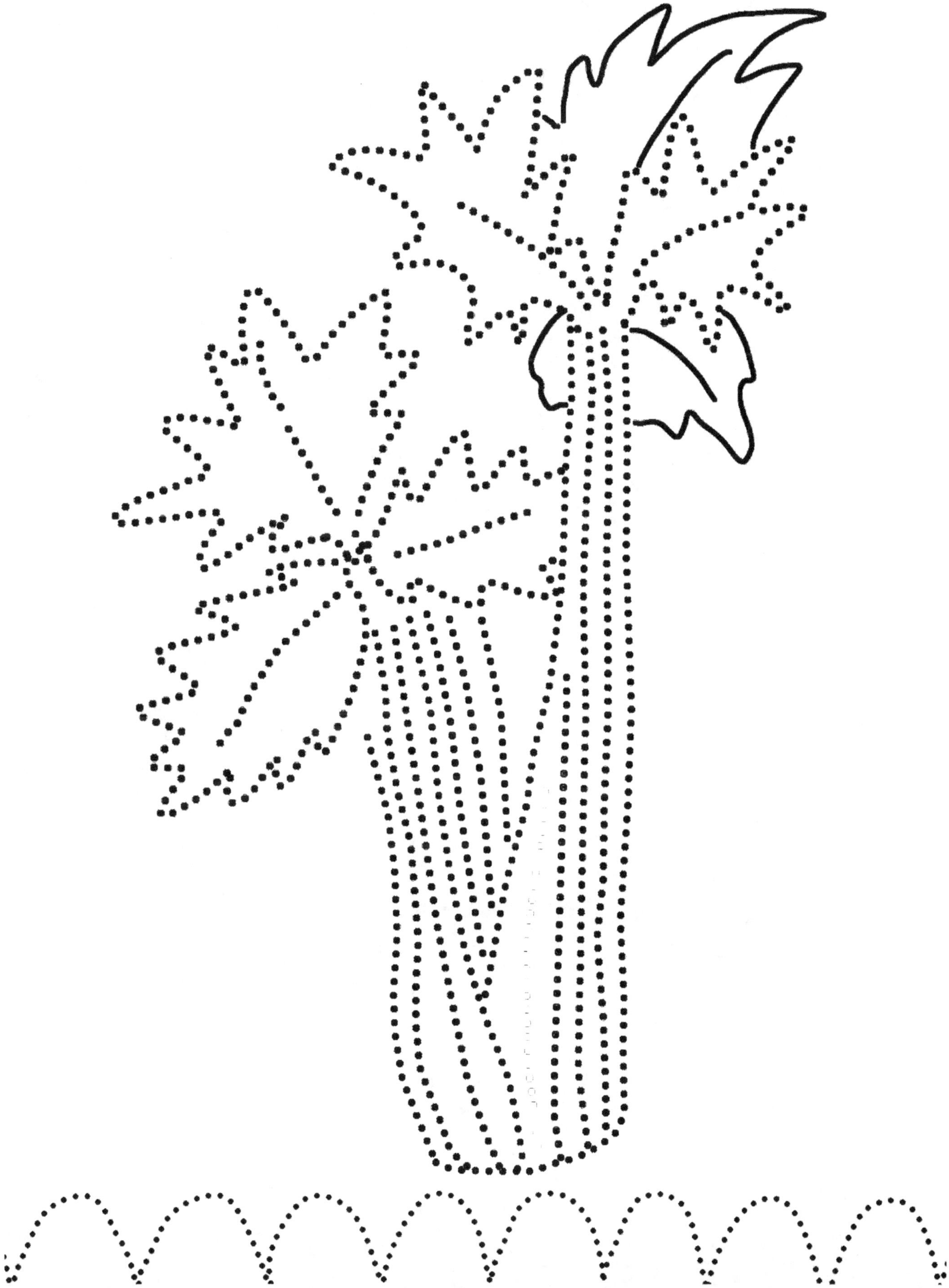

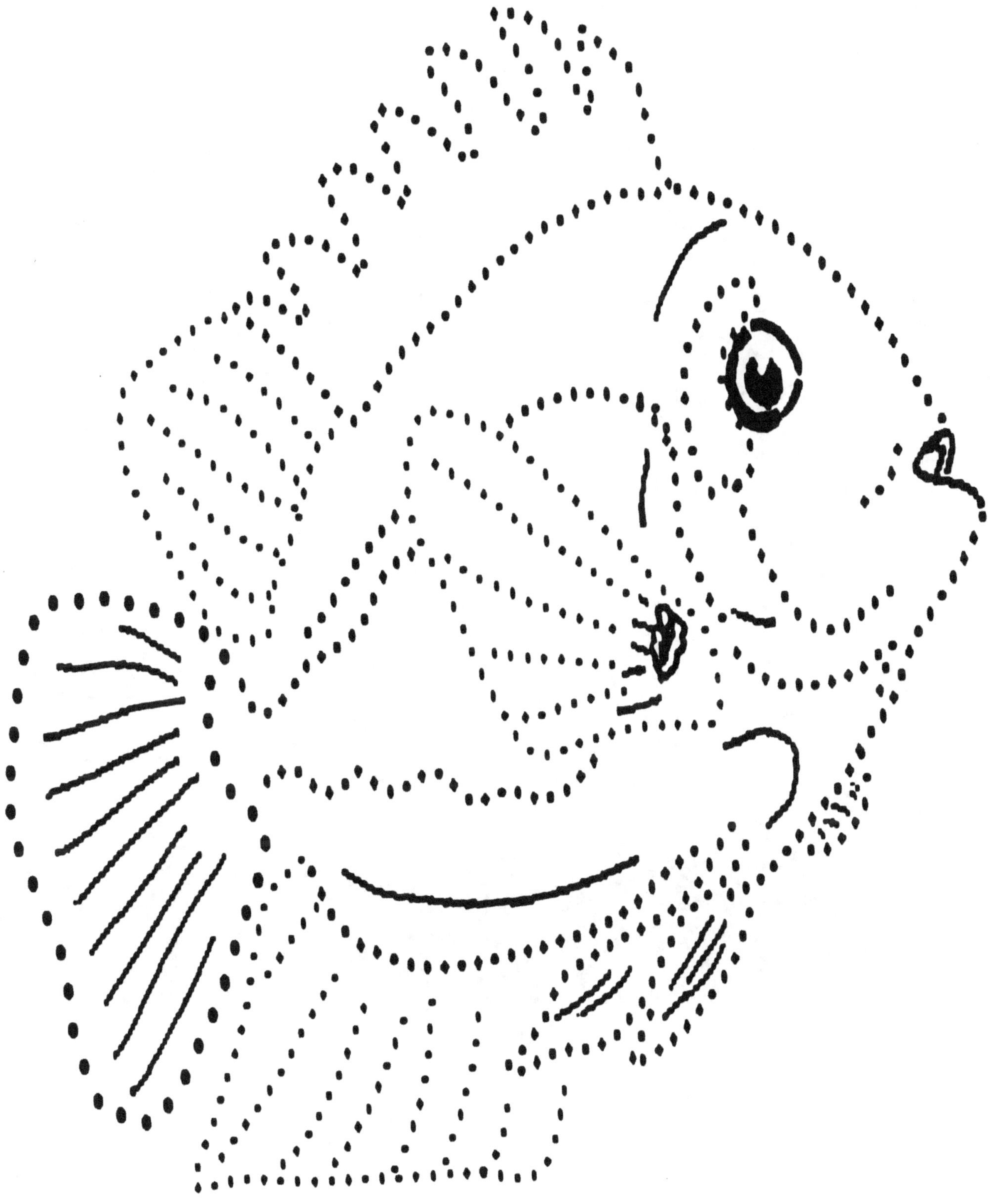

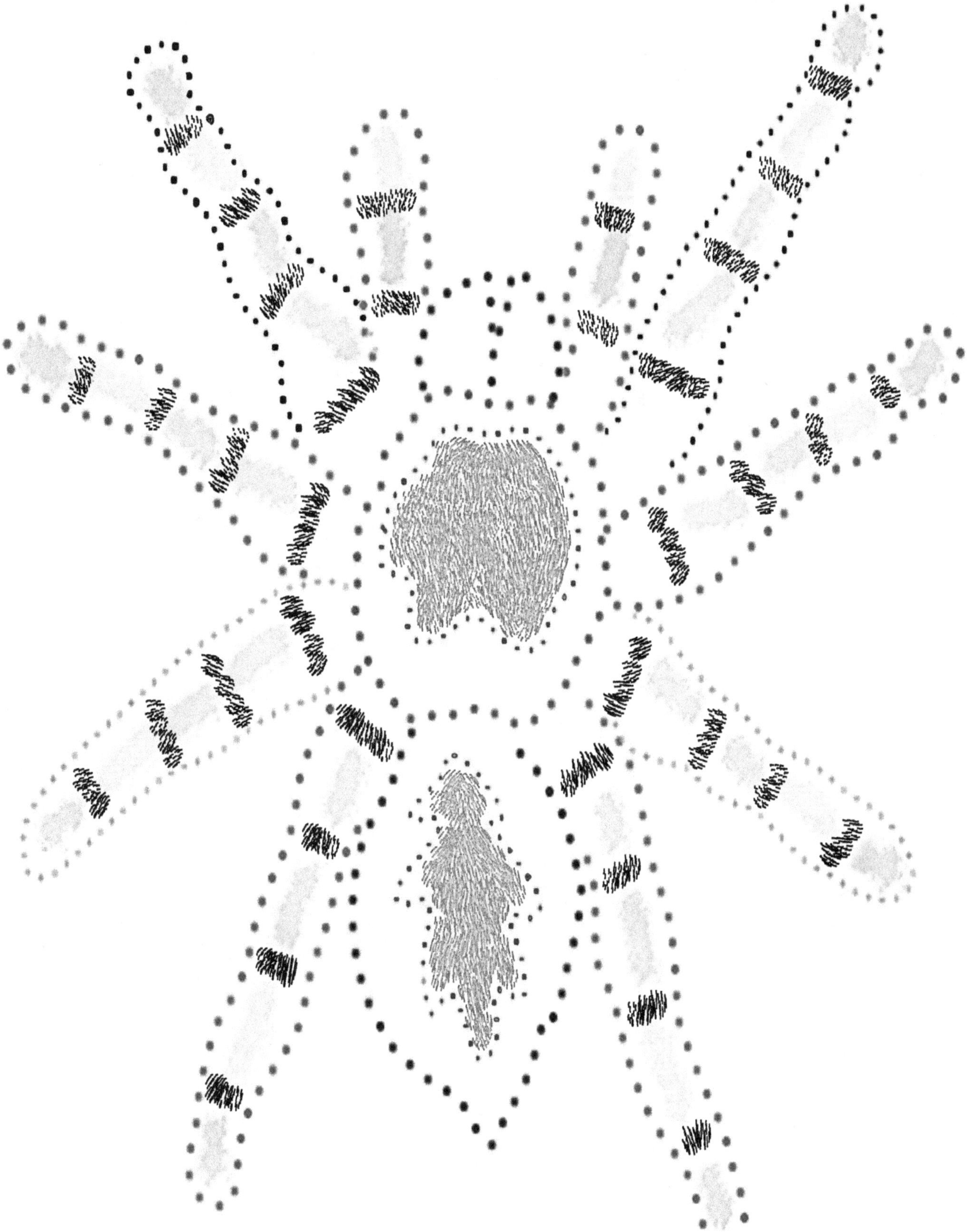

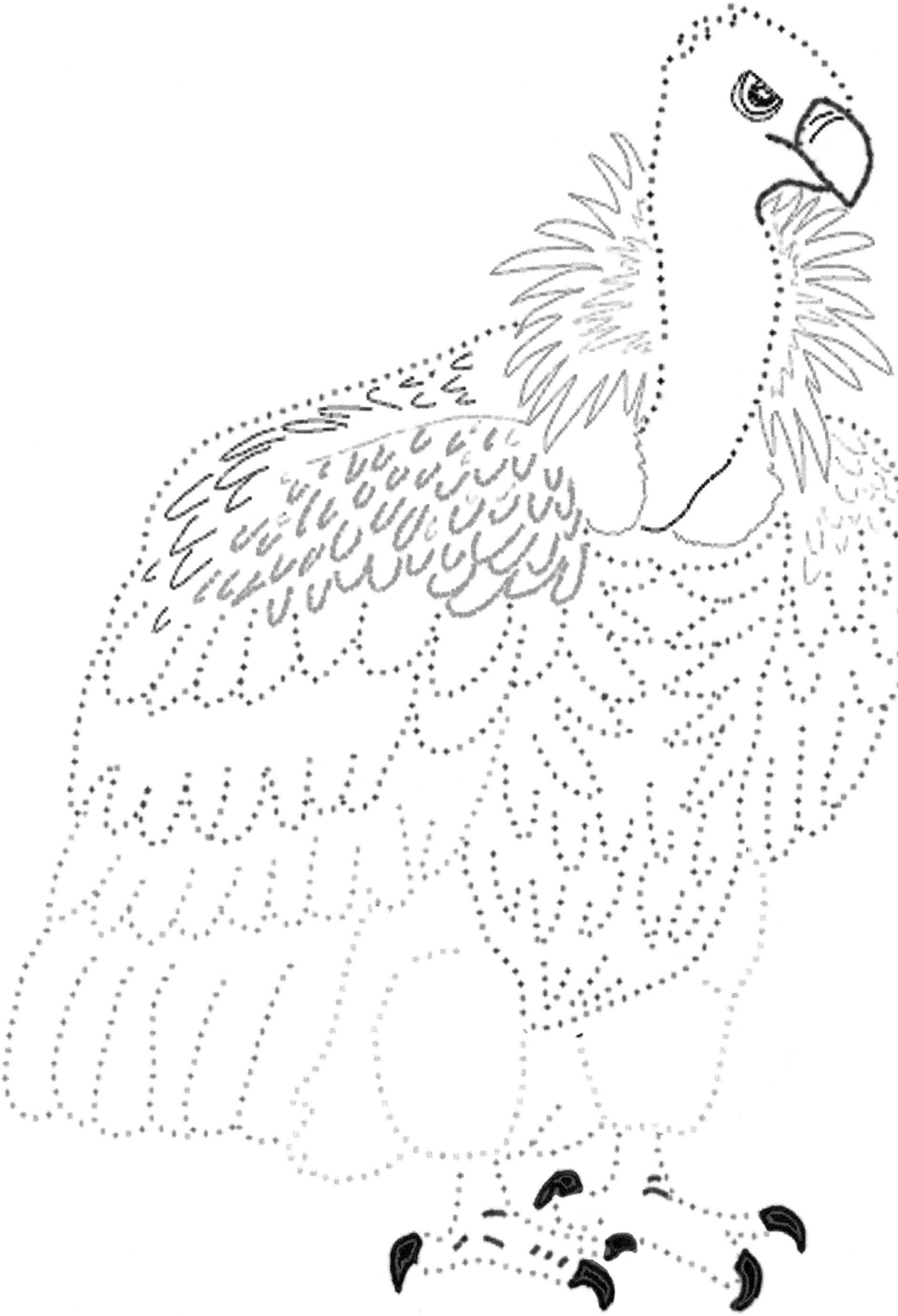

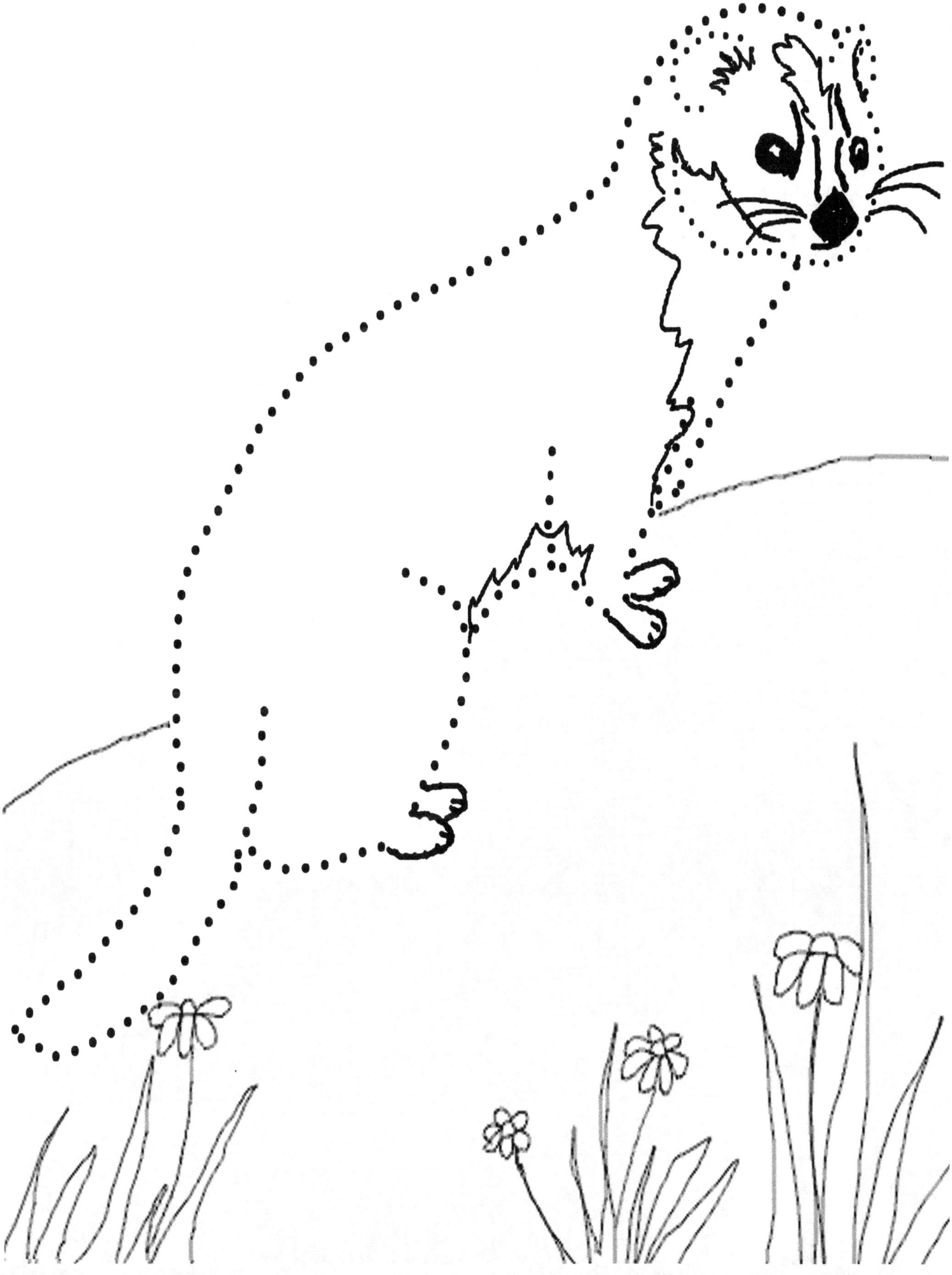

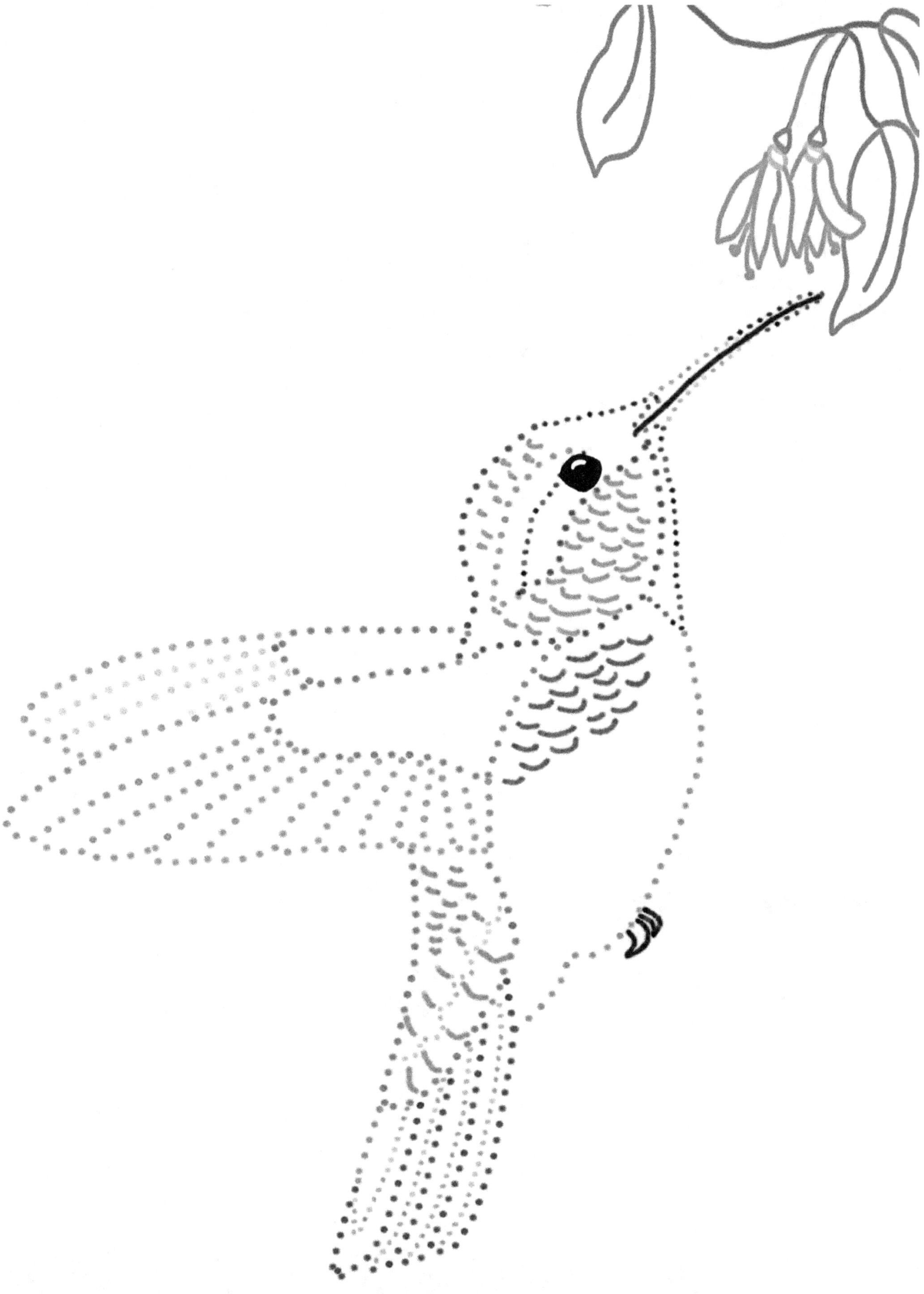

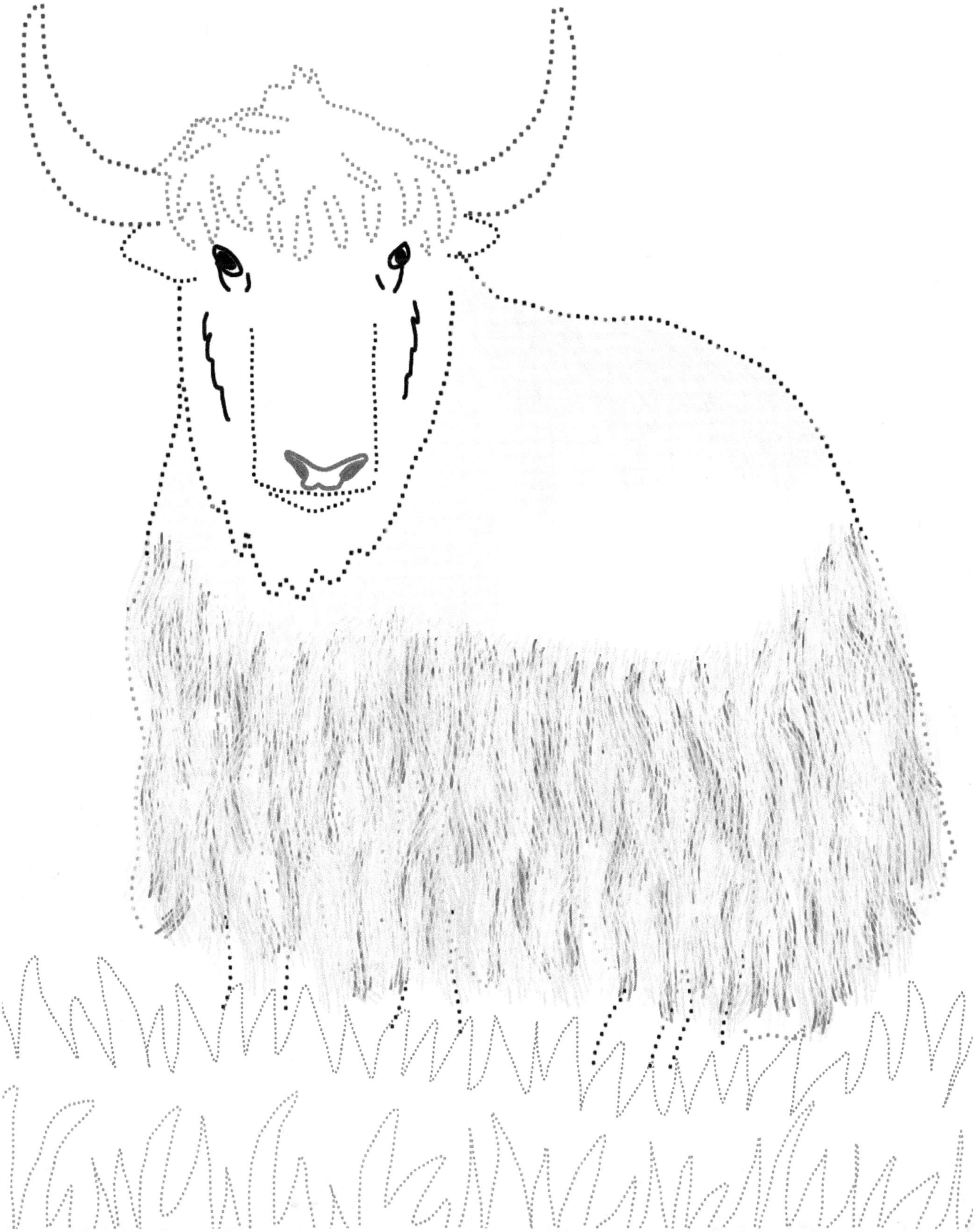

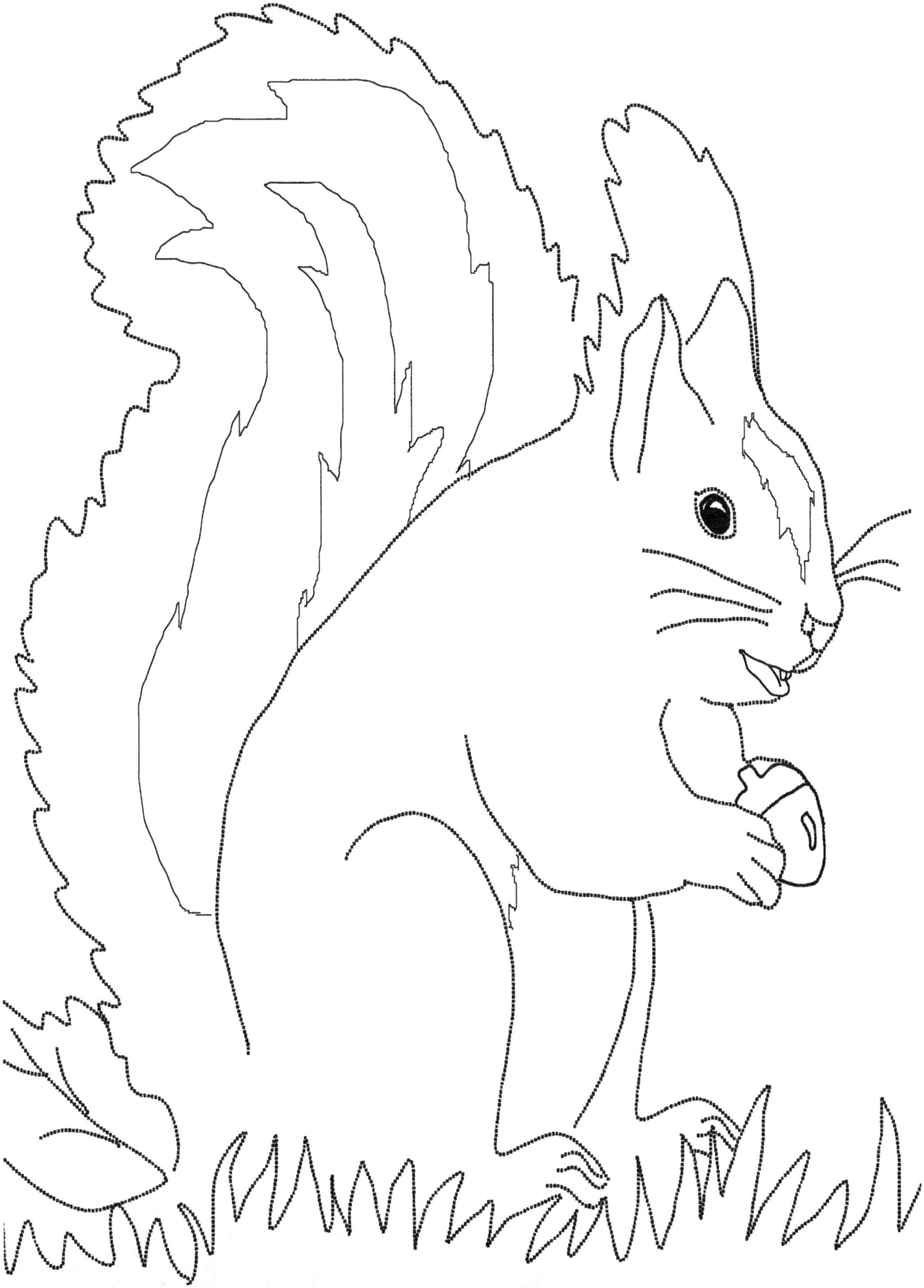

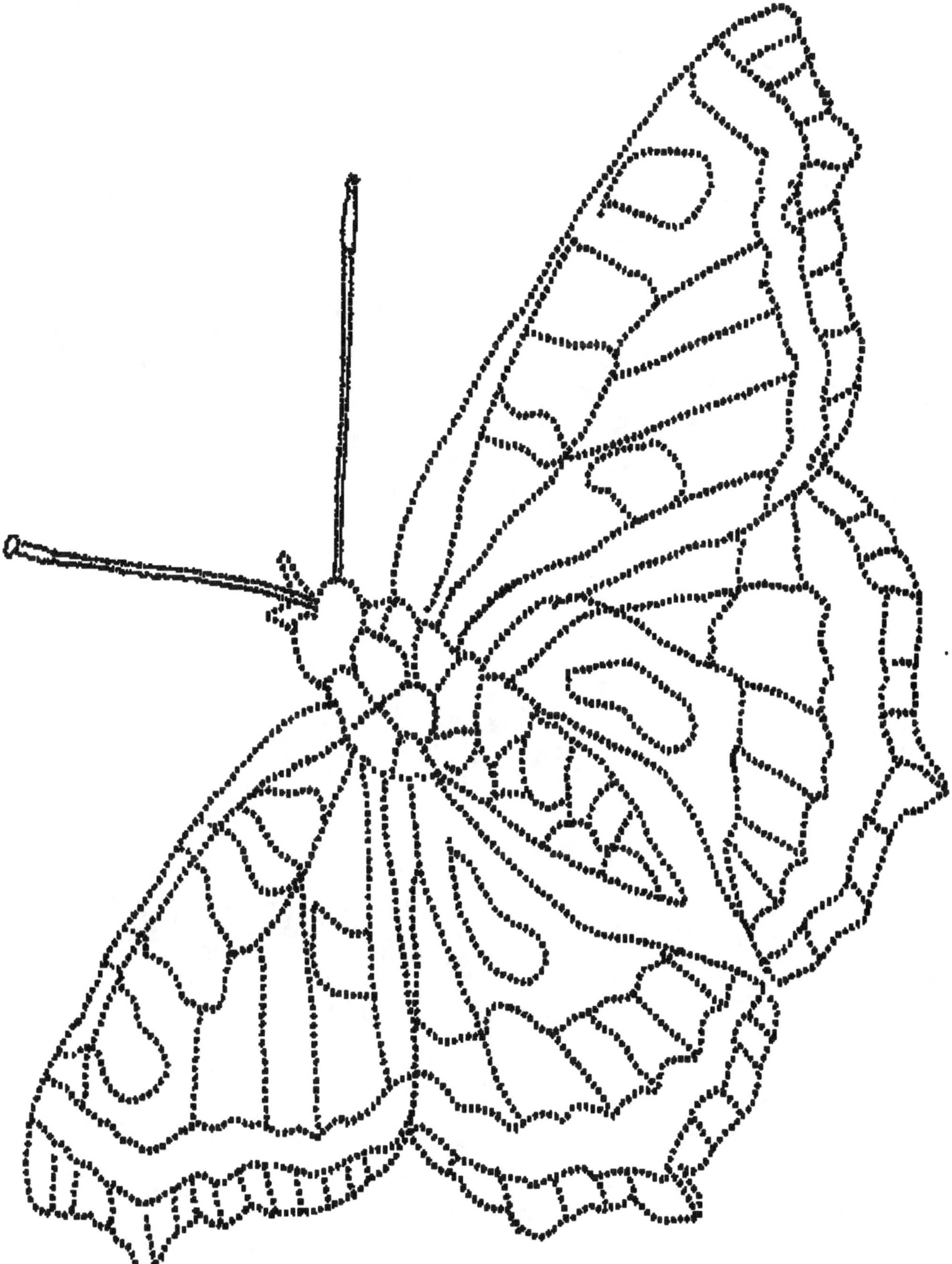

www.ingramcontent.com/pod-product-compliance
Lightning Source LLC
Chambersburg PA
CBHW081747220526
45468CB00008B/2270
* 9 7 8 1 7 2 3 0 4 0 9 0 0 *